THE CELTIC QUEST

The Celtic Quest:
A Contemporary Spirituality

Rosemary Power

the columba press

First published in 2010 by
the columba press
55A Spruce Avenue, Stillorgan Industrial Park,
Blackrock, Co Dublin

Cover by Bill Bolger
Origination by The Columba Press
Printed in Ireland by ColourBooks Ltd, Dublin

ISBN 978 1 85607 698-2

Contents

Foreword

A book of this kind can only skim the surface of something as wide-ranging as Celtic spirituality, with all it social, theological and spiritual implications, and this book is intended only as a relatively short commentary. There are many more questions than answers, more suggestions than definitions and whole areas that have not been touched upon.

The purpose is to explore how Celtic Christianity has developed in recent decades, its sources and their uses, and the part it has played in contemporary Christian spirituality. It has grown out of many discussions and the contributions, critique and support of numerous friends and colleagues. Thanks are due to in particular to Sheila and Anne Crotty who showed me how music can bring a deeper perspective, to members and associates of the Iona Community, to Jenny Meegan, Kay Muhr, Brian Lambkin, Des Bain, and to all who have contributed, whether or not they agree with the approach I have taken. Special thanks for help with exploring the theological aspects are due to Professor Alan Ford and Dr Alison Millbank at the University of Nottingham. Professor Donald Meek has generously shared of his extensive knowledge, and Cathy Swift has provided some valuable historical insights. This book is dedicated to the memory of Alice Reilly.

I write from the perspective of sympathy towards modern Celtic Christianity, as a participant-observer of Christianity, from some knowledge of both the medieval literary and the more recent folk traditions, especially in Ireland, as a Member of one of the groups studied, the Iona Community, and as someone who has engaged in Celtic spirituality events. A certain amount of what follows is drawn from personal conversations with many individuals in these different contexts, and participation at and facilitation of 'Celtic' devotional events. Any errors of fact or interpretation are my own.

CHAPTER ONE

Setting the scene

Introduction

'Celtic spirituality' of all kinds is very popular. We can read books about it, go on courses, conferences, retreats and pilgrimages, we can buy 'Celtic' jewellery and 'Celtic' music, we can burn 'Celtic' candles and partake in 'Celtic' rituals to welcome the seasons. We can browse through websites which can initiate us into 'Celtic' Christian renewal or ancient Welsh Wicca. The possibilities seem endless.

The writings we associate with Celtic spirituality have become deeply rooted, and they are accepted by many people as a native expression of Christianity, a part of the heritage of Ireland, Scotland, Wales, and also of England. Celtic spirituality has been with us for the last twenty-five years, and gives pleasure and a sense of spiritual fulfilment to many people, particularly through beautiful works of medieval literature and folk poetry which have found a wide and appreciative audience.

Modern Celtic spirituality is based on a relatively small number of early medieval texts and a collection of late nineteenth-century folk poetry, though the movement has constantly reinterpreted and rewritten these resources, finding new applications for them and producing its own poetry, prose and interpretations 'in the Celtic tradition'. Most writers on Celtic spirituality rely on translations, or their own or others' adaptations, and the extent to which they are 'Celtic' is not always obvious. At its best, Celtic spirituality seems to fill a real need and, whether or not historically true, it has developed in its own right. However, it is also true that much of what is called Celtic is derived from what others have written, often known at third hand, which has then been cited as fact, or adapted by new writers. Either way it is worth considering how and why this has happened, to learn more about how Celtic spirituality has developed, why it is so important at present, and how, in spite of these drawbacks, it remains so attractive.

Both modern Christian and pagan Celtic spirituality seem to have developed at much the same time, in the late twentieth century, as part of a movement sometimes called the 'new Celtic Twilight'. There are similarities between the pagan and Christian manifestations in the focus on individual personal development and the growth of one's inner spiritual capabilities. The Christian version, however, while it has specific emphases, is almost always orthodox in terms of mainstream Christian belief.

What we now call Celtic spirituality has little in common with what is normally taught in a university department of Celtic Studies. A full study of the material would require knowledge of the cultures of these islands from the second century to the twentieth; acquaintance with the academic disciples of literature, history, folklore, archaeology, theology and church history; and a working familiarity with the Irish and Welsh languages in all their forms from ancient to modern, Scottish Gaelic, Old English and Latin. The roots of the Christian movement have been explored by a handful of scholars, and the development of pagan forms of Celtic spirituality have also been considered by scholars writing from the point of view of folk tradition. This book will not attempt to cover the historical background or the literary and theological contributions of early Christianity in these islands.

The term 'Celtic' is used here because that is how people who use the books produced by the movement think about it. It refers to what people think they are doing, what they are creating and believe they are reconstructing, rather than whether it can be justified historically. Celtic spirituality is worth considering in its own right because it contains a distinctive approach to modern issues in contemporary western Christianity. Celtic spirituality is accepted as real, in particular by the spiritually-inclined white middle classes with expendable income, part of a social group which had rarely been a regarded as a repository of popular culture, but may be as capable of contributing as any other group.

This book will explore Celtic spirituality as a movement that rose in the later twentieth century in response to spiritual needs of the time, and was seen at first as a means by which people who had discovered and enjoyed certain religious poems could use them as a tool for mission and church growth, making their faith attractive in a fresh way to a wide range of people. Several gifted writers started the movement for these purposes, and many others followed suit.

This book asks how it has developed, who it is used by and what concerns are expressed through the use of the 'Celtic'. This will involve a consideration of how supposedly Celtic themes were acquired and in what circumstances; how they are translated and interpreted; what has been rejected by the original selectors and may be unknown to contemporary practitioners; and what has been dropped by them and why. The creation of powerful images, and the emphasis on community life, liturgy and hymnody, have all had an effect on the movement. We will also look at the relationships between key themes interpreted from medieval or folk material; whether modern Celtic spirituality is limited by the level of content that can be regarded as true to the original sources, and the extent to which any such limitation may hinder the readers' spirituality. Finally, there will be a few suggestions on ways in which the movement could incorporate traditional material that has not yet been used.

We will concentrate on the written word because this seems central to modern Celtic spirituality. The emphasis will be on why people are interpreting texts in a particular manner; how the modern readings of the texts have acquired a dynamic of their own; the concerns which are interpreted through a 'Celtic' medium as specific themes; and the effect that the individual interpretations have on later readers who in turn contribute to the movement. This means that we will look mainly at the books, and the recent websites, of the movement, and the use of the 'Celtic' in talks and religious services. While we will try to cover the main themes that have emerged, only a few of the wide range of contemporary books on the subject will be included. We will not be able to consider except in passing the importance of art and the value placed on designs derived from the great Gospel books, whose iconography we are only beginning to understand again. Another, important, area that cannot be covered here is the lack of relationship between modern Celtic spirituality and contemporary folk music, a subject that needs a book to it-

self. The development of a specific Welsh form of the movement, the response of academics, pagan Celtic spirituality and
the growth of dispersed and residential communities other than
Iona, are areas we can cover only in passing. This means that
substantial aspects of the current Celtic spirituality movement
will not be considered at all in this short introduction, but it will
be possible to look briefly at some of the effects of Celtic spirituality on wider Christian experience over the last twenty years,
and its social, theological and spiritual concerns.

There are theological questions that need to be considered
because we need to ask why Celtic spirituality has developed at
this particular time and has effected a wide variety of people, including on those undecided, uncommitted or in the process of
leaving church life. Some of the reasons may reflect changes in
society, and the decline in influence, wealth and numbers in the
Christian churches. Others may reflect increased levels of formal
education and personal decision-making among church-goers;
and others the emphasis in the last forty years on spiritual development through individual or group retreats. There is also
the question of the growth of an audience acquainted with the
contemporary Celtic movement through its literature, inputs at
religious conferences, and new liturgies, and of how it came
about that the prevailing understanding of 'Celtic' religious activity is considered an alternative or an addition to more established forms of religious practice.

One of the many paradoxes of the movement is that it came
into being not in the countries that historically spoke the Celtic
languages, but in the north of England, in areas that had no
native Celtic heritage or Celtic language. From the start, and
mainly through the work of English evangelicals, ancient and
relatively recent poems and prose excerpts in the Celtic languages have been presented as part of a tradition common to
both islands. Ancient English prayers, and most of its native
poetry and prose was discarded, except for the seventh-century
writer Bede's great Latin work, *The Ecclesiastical History of the
English People*. In spite of its title, this is a much-loved work that
has been presented as Celtic because it tells in a digestible way
of the early stages of the conversion of England to Christianity,
and contains many anecdotes, similar to stories found in Irish

and Welsh saints' lives. These can be used as parables to entertain and explain the effects of faith in the lives of the early followers of Christianity, or at least the more prominent ones. Indeed,
in making the Celtic apply to England too, some authors, like the
poet David Adam, have claimed that the sixth-century inhabitants of northern England, to whom the works of Bede refer, were
a Celtic remnant and possibly already Christian.

The modern understanding of the 'Celtic', then, sits rather
lightly with the known source material, and is almost entirely
dependent on translations. This is true not only of England but
also of Ireland, Wales and Scotland, the traditional heartlands of
the Celtic languages and cultures, which in turn have also
adopted versions of modern Celtic spirituality. Most of the
translations used were made in the late nineteenth and early
twentieth centuries as a result of the extensive collecting and
artistic activity connected with the nineteenth-century Celtic
Twilight, and more recent translators and commentators do not
necessarily understand the 'Celtic' in the same way as these collectors and translators. In spite of this heavy dependence on
works influenced by the climate of an earlier age, these same
translations have made it possible to overcome linguistic and
cultural divides, and they are used in England as part of a process
regarded as 'recovering' ancient native tradition. In Ireland and
Wales the movement is more one that identifies itself as providing continuity with the native culture.

This brings us to a theological question, the extent to which
an interpretation that is factually wrong, or at least misunder-
stood, incomplete and distorted, can yet be a source of spiritual
growth and engagement. We need to consider in terms of contemporary theology the possibility that God may respond to
historically naïve spirituality as positively as to the historically
verifiable. This means we also need to reflect on the theological
responsibility of the practitioners, writers, speakers and retreat-
givers to represent the genuine texts and their intrinsic theology
and spirituality, and their responsibility to leave evidence of
where to find the elements they discard, as these may have
value to some readers at the present time, and possibly to future
readers as well.

Defining Celtic spirituality

While a later chapter will consider the themes and images of the movement, we need to identify here some of the defining attributes of modern Celtic Christianity. It usually includes some or all of the following elements:

- An emphasis on orthodox Christian doctrine, in particular that of the Trinity, as known through translations of ancient or nineteenth-century Gaelic and Welsh folk poetry and their modern derivatives.
- An interest in nature, seasonal practices and the experience of the divine as immanent. Closely connected is a desire to respect the environment.
- A sense of place, linked to a desire for travel, expressed as pilgrimage.
- A belief that the ancient Celtic peoples lived in harmony with the natural world, and with each other.
- A belief that Celtic spirituality is holistic, all-encompassing and relevant for every aspect of daily life and work.
- A belief in the spontaneity of the ancient Celts as expressed in worship, lack of structure and perceived liturgical freedom; and a distrust of ecclesiastical structures.
- A certainty of the equality of women in the early 'Celtic Church'.
- The importance of art, in designs, dance, music and forms of self-expression, often incorporated into liturgy.
- The importance of telling stories about, and applying the lives of the 'Celtic' saints, including English saints, as models for today.
- A conviction that the Celtic is the ancient and recoverable heritage of the people of these islands, including for English writers, the English.
- A sense of liminality, of being on the edge, spiritually and organisationally, and an enjoyment of the experience.

Not all these features, several of which were previously identified by Mark Atherton (2002), are always present, and the movement is full of paradoxes. Some works disassociate themselves from some of the themes we have just outlined, and some even from the notion itself. For example, Fay Sampson's *Visions and Voyages* (1998), states there was no such thing as Celtic spirituality, but then addresses it as if it does exist .

One of the themes that is met again and again is the sense of liminality, of the Celtic being on the edges. This is certainly how Saint Patrick viewed Ireland, on the western edge of the known world, outside the structures of the Roman Empire. His understanding has become embedded in a movement which sees the Celtic Fringe as geographically and culturally marginal, a world of wild coastlines, physically on the edge of Europe, which can be the focus for travel, physical and spiritual, and which provides a sense of arrival at what is different and yet familiar. This being on the edge is a statement of what the Celtic is thought to be, containing the sense of excitement, difference, adventure and recovery of something precious and fragile, preserved on the edges. Such elements appear again and again in books of the current movement. What is there on the edges is important enough to bring back and share, in its pristine and unsullied form. What we find there can open doors that reunite us to the past and give us new ways of seeing old truths.

This is a response that touches the emotions, and current books about Celtic spirituality often appear to distrust intellectuals, and to see their approach as narrow and dry, while the writers themselves avoid a rigorous approach to the sources. As we have seen, some of its original English proponents viewed Celtic spirituality as native English heritage. They believed that it was severely damaged at the Synod of Whitby in 664 when the 'Celtic Church', which is usually regarded as highly individualistic, but on this subject is treated as if it were a single unity, lost out to a centralised 'Roman Church'. It is believed that this Northumbrian event, depicted three generations later by Bede, had an effect on the church in all the Celtic lands, which eventually capitulated to Roman authority.

This predominantly English approach was developed mainly by theologically conservative Anglicans, nearly all clergymen, who tend to view Celtic spirituality as a tool for renewal and church growth. The writers of this English form usually assumed that, in spite of the difference in language, they were rediscovering their own 'Celtic' roots. They often give the impression that England was as culturally and politically dominant in early

Christian times as it was later, though there is a crucial difference in that they see the focal point as Northumbria rather than
London.

The distrust of intellectual approaches, and emphasis on the
emotive, can be seen in many of the books about Celtic spirituality that include stories about ancient saints and their actions.
These books sometimes also contain stories about contemporary
events. In both cases the use of 'narrative theology', of express-
ing the major beliefs of Christianity through storytelling, may
account for this approach. The writers have often struggled to
find ways in which the stories could sit less oddly with our present concerns and some have adapted them freely, possibility
taking them very far from what the original writers or their
audience thought they expressed.

Another interesting aspect of the movement is that the key
writers often combined their involvement with a distrust of formal ecclesiastical structures, yet many of the Christian organisations that espouse Celtic spirituality are highly structured and
place a strong emphasis on determining where spiritual authority
lies.

A recognisable Irish variant of Celtic Christianity has developed, largely in response to the Northumbria-based movement,
and perhaps to a sense that the 'Celtic' was being culturally hi-
jacked. This version displays a greater sense of ease and continuity with Ireland's cultural inheritance, including much that is
neither specifically pagan nor Christian. It represents itself as recovering what has survived at the fringe, in a Gaelic context,
with the implication that this is more genuine than the English
version. This approach was taken by John Ó Ríordáin (1996) and
can be found in a work we will consider later, a collection of native folk tradition, writings on the church Fathers and personal
reflections by the poet John O'Donohue (1954-2007).

Some of the early proponents of modern Celtic Christianity
used the early Welsh Lives of the Saints and poetry from the
early Middle Ages, and this was taken up in Wales, in particular
in places associated with ancient rituals, such as holy wells.
Scotland, however, was relatively late in claiming a part in
Celtic Christianity. This gives us another paradox as in parts of
the Highlands and Western Islands a Celtic language is still

spoken and the folk tradition has to some extent been preserved. Also, a major resource in the development of Celtic Christianity was the English translation of the *Carmina Gadelica*, the late-nineteenth-century collection of Hebridean oral poetry, much of it specifically religious, made by Alexander Carmichael (1832-1912) and first published in six volumes between 1900 and 1971. The movement has shown great interest in the written word, which is portable and adaptable, but very little in the local cultures of the people still living in areas which have a native heritage that can be considered Celtic.

Another kind of Scottish influence can be traced through the Iona Community, founded in mid-twentieth-century Scotland and often viewed from outside as a home of Celtic spirituality. There is considerable interest in Iona, both the island and the Community, particularly in terms of a sense of place, essentially a spiritual homeland. This seems to speak to a desire often expressed for new ways of belonging, to a place as well as to a group, and has led to ancient places associated with early Christianity, Holy Island (Lindisfarne), Bradwell-on-Sea and others, but most of all Iona, becoming destinations for journeys, physical and metaphorical, into Celtic spirituality.

Another important feature is how theologically orthodox the modern Christian movement is. It has a strong focus on the Trinity, and while emphasising the immanent presence of God in the individual and in the surrounding world, it never loses a sense of the transcendent. There is a particular concern with relations between humans and the natural world, and this leads to an emphasis on nature poetry, seasonal poetry and the rhythms of daily life, all of which are used with the expectation of experiencing God in and through the world around. Most of the books say that this is how the ancient Celts experienced God, but the emphasis on God immanent is a growing aspect of contemporary Christian theology in general, and it may be that this is being read into the past.

This is an example both of exegesis, the study of the interpretation of scripture or other religious texts in order to discern what the original meaning was for the writer and audience, but also of *eisegesis*, the interpretation by an individual or group based on their own or their collective experience. In the case of the early Christian texts used in modern Celtic spirituality, we know little of the practices, and still less the inner beliefs of the warrior peoples of earlier times, and the spiritual commentaries that have survived from early Ireland are little used by the movement. In the case of the folk traditions, the way of life that formed them is alien to most of contemporary society. Personal or group interpretations have dominated how we present Celtic spirituality today. This brings us to one of the weaknesses of the movement, that people may find what they seek, and possibly what they want, rather than what actually existed. In either case, their starting point is in contemporary Christianity rather than the faith which formed the writings they use.

The movement is also orthodox in terms of spirituality. This is a difficult concept to define but the word is used in this book with regard to a sense of inner cohesion, a place of growth that is independent of skills, life opportunities or inherent gifts, but which can accommodate all of these within a relationship with the divine. The relationship, which involves a divine presence external to the individual, is an unequal one and it involves the individual seeking the will of the divine, and in Christian terms to enter more and more into the community of the divine.

Oliver Davies, in his 1996 book *Celtic Spirituality in Early Medieval Wales*, gives his understanding:

> Although this is a word that lacks precise meaning, it can be said – in its Christian context – to embrace the church in both its visible and invisible aspects and to suggest a complex of theological ideas, sacramental experience, religious forms of life and interior piety that construct Christian experience at a particular time and place. Within such an ecclesial context, spirituality can be defined as active and personal disciple-ship in Christ at all levels of our being. (1996, 2-3)

While this is a fairly formal and ecclesial interpretation, most people who espouse the Christian form of Celtic spirituality more or less accept traditional Christian concepts of spirituality, even if their faith and engagement with a worshipping community may be strained. Some of the Christian adherents may be influenced by aspects of modern Pagan Celtic spirituality, which takes many forms but in general has a tendency to accept pantheism, place a stronger emphasis on responsibility for one's personal self-improvement, and expect a more equal relationship with the divine.

To return to the mainstream Celtic spirituality movement, it is, in most forms, a twentieth-century orthodox Christian *fin-de-siècle* movement, which drew on the increasing availability of certain texts from Gaelic and medieval literature, and even more from nineteenth-century Gaelic oral tradition. These sources have been supplemented by contemporary creative works, and together have created a corpus which is seen as recovering a native tradition.

We may also need to consider that it developed first in Britain at a time when British society was changing fast, when its sense of communality appeared to be under threat, and when there was increasing disillusionment with, and resistance to, traditional institutions. These included the churches, which were seen as being out of touch with contemporary spiritual needs and social expectations.

We will consider how the movement developed, its ability to take a wide range of material on board and then to weed out certain contributions, leaving a common core of works people have found useful. Many of the 'Celtic' books popular in the 1980s and 1990s have vanished without trace. Some have vanished but left traces, and it is worth looking at how some books came to be accepted while others were abandoned. What emerged as 'Celtic' was what was seen as a creative, holistic, unifying, earthy, endorsing an environmentally-responsible relational spirituality that addressed a desire for beauty in worship and private devotion. In order to look at how this happened, we need to consider what these sources were.

CHAPTER TWO

Celts then and now:
The sources of the movement

Who were the Celts?

To understand how Celtic spirituality has developed, we need to consider briefly what was known about the early Christians in Britain and Ireland and how it was adapted to allow the development in the late twentieth century.

Many books on Celtic spirituality contain some information on the early Celtic peoples, sometimes as background to the lives of the saints, and sometimes to explain what are seen as tensions in relation to continental Christianity. While the folk tradition has been rather neglected, there are a number of general overviews of the early Christian period, including Leslie Hardinge's *The Celtic Church in Britain* (1972) and Kathleen Hughes' and Ann Hamlin's *The Modern Traveller to the Early Irish Church* (1977). Máire Herbert's *Iona, Kells and Derry* (1988, 1996) is a standard scholarly work on the history of the monasteries associated with Saint Columba, while Colmán Etchingham's *Church organisation in Ireland, AD 650 to 1000* (1999) gives background to how the church in Ireland was structured in the period when most of the poems, saints' lives and other prose we use were written. Other academic works worth consulting include Michael Richter's *The Formation of the Medieval West* for the European context (1994, 181-230), Michael Herrin and Shirley Ann Brown's *Christ in Celtic Christianity: Britain and Ireland from the Fifth to the Tenth Century* (2002), and Kim McCone's *Pagan Past and Christian Present in Early Irish Literature* (2000).

Some academic writers now include an introductory section addressing the contemporary interpretations of their subject from the point of view of Celtic spirituality. These include Christina Harrington's *Women in a Celtic Church: Ireland 450-1150* (2002, 9-16), Caitlin Corning's *The Celtic and Roman tradi-*

tions: conflict and consensus in the early medieval church (2006, 2-18), and John Blair's *The Church in Anglo-Saxon Society* (2005).

Other academic writers both comment on the movement and contribute to it. They include Oliver Davies (1996), who specialises in early Welsh material, John Carey (1999), who worked on the early Irish material, and a number of the writers edited by Dauvit Broun and Thomas Clancy in their anthology on Saint Columba (1999) who concentrated on the Scottish aspects. Other academics who have studied the movement from an academic perspective include the Scot Donald Meek (2000), who was born on the Gaelic-speaking island of Tiree, the Irish Thomas O'Loughlin, who wrote both an academic and a popular book on Celtic spirituality (2000a, 2000b), and Douglas Dales (1997) who concentrated on missionary theology on both islands, and writes from within the movement. England and Anglo-Saxon spirituality were considered by Paul Cavill (1999) who, while aware of modern concepts, approaches them by giving evidence relating to his period rather than by addressing them directly. Useful historical summaries also accompany some modern translations. D. H. Farmer's introduction to four key Anglo-Saxon texts, *The Age of Bede,* was published in 1965, before the modern movement had started, while Richard Sharpe's introduction to *Adomnám's Life of St Columba* (1991) was written as it grew.

The work of these writers touches, depending on their scholarly focus, on Celtic tribes as linguistic and cultural groupings; their arrival in these islands; the coming of Christianity; its retention in the cultural heartlands; its spread, in particular through the monastic bases of Iona and Lindisfarne; and the extent to which church organisation and local theology differed from the practice and belief of the universal church.

Many of the writers of books on popular Celtic spirituality have given their own interpretations of early Christianity in both Britain and Ireland, with varying degrees of selectivity and accuracy (Sampson 1998, Ellis and Seaton 1998, Olsen 2003). These, rather than the academic works, have influenced other writers, and have led to the popularisation of some of the central themes of modern Celtic spirituality.

Historical background
While 'Celtic' is used in this book to mean what the current movement understands it to mean, the term is mostly used by scholars to refer to the group of related languages, which survive in Ireland, the western Highlands and Islands of Scotland, and in a revived form in the Isle of Man; in Wales, Brittany and in a revived form in Cornwall. Legal systems, literature and some cultural aspects of family organisation, land-ownership and even art forms are associated with these areas and are frequently referred to as Celtic.

While the use of the term 'Celtic' at all is disputed by some contemporary academics, it remains in use for a group of tribes that dominated the west of Europe in classical times, and were described by the Roman writer Tacitus as one of the three great peoples of the world. Spreading westward in several waves they took up residence in both Britain and Ireland in the centuries before Christ, and established themselves as the ruling warrior classes. While their language, culture and artefacts became dominant, they may well have always been minorities, mingling with earlier inhabitants in the areas they settled, and adopting their habits and culture.

Christianity came to what is now known as England in the second century through the Roman Empire, of which it was part. As the Roman Empire withdrew in the fourth and fifth centuries, new settlers of Germanic origin arrived across the North Sea. Christianity appears to have survived, though with limited structures, in the western areas that remained the most Romanised, and in Galloway where the later Candida Casa of St Ninian seems to have been a focal point. In the fifth century a boy from western Britain, Patrick, was taken as a slave to Ireland, later escaped or was freed, and studied on the Continent. He then returned to Ireland, and was the major force in making Christianity, which had been a minority religion, the undisputed faith of the island, something which happened within about two generations. Patrick's autobiography and a letter by him have survived, and he was frequently referred to by later writers.

There were certain specific characteristics shared by the early church in Ireland and the church that survived in what we now call Wales. Neither had the civic structure of the Roman Empire which the church had mirrored on the continent, and Ireland was the first country north-west of the Roman Empire to receive Christianity. The normal continental pattern of bishops with oversight for an area, and ordained presbyters, was used, but otherwise church organisation tended to mirror the culture it found itself in, a culture of small settlements and local tribal rule. It developed a monastic focus, patterned to some extent on the monastic communities of the early church in North Africa. Within a short period, numerous monasteries were founded, many of which were bound together by allegiance to a common founder, but which functioned independently. A few of these seem to have survived as late as the sixteenth-century Reformation, at Glendalough in the Wicklow mountains, and at Devenish Island in County Fermanagh where the site was shared with a medieval continental order of monks.

Some women's monasteries were also established in the early years of Christianity, the most famous of which was the double monastery at Kildare. Women's foundations are on the whole not well recorded, tended to be short-lived. and were hampered because it was nearly impossible in Irish society of the time for women to own land.

Another feature was that, although the earliest sources are in Latin, the language of the universal church, writing in the vernacular, the native language, appeared at an early time and was used for both religious and secular works. Christianity in England was to adopt this practice of writing in the native language as well as Latin.

The new religion was strengthened on the west coast of Scotland, which had been settled from Ireland, by the establishment on the island of Iona of a major monastery. This was founded by a member of one of Ireland's ruling dynasties, the monk known as Colum Cille, in Latin Columba. Iona rapidly became a major centre of learning, the head of the *familia*, the loose federation of monasteries associated with Columba. Though later damaged by Viking raids, it was to remain significant, was re-founded as a Benedictine monastery, and thrived until the Reformation.

Apart from making Iona a centre for prayer, writing and pilgrimage, Columba also undertook diplomatic activities from it that brought him into contact with the Pictish royal family. Later, his monastery hosted exiles from Northumbria, and the links forged in both cases led to the spread of Christianity to different races and cultures with different languages.

The Northumbria mission is exceptionally important to the modern movement. While there are other sources for Ireland, including Patrick's writings and the evidence that can be drawn from the writings produced at the monastic *scriptorium* on Iona, the main, and most popular, source for the conversion of Britain is the account by the seventh-century Northumbrian monk Bede, whose Germanic forebears had themselves converted to Christianity not many generations previously. As recorded by Bede, a mission was led in the seventh century, after a brief false start, by Aidan, a monk of Iona, who was given the tidal island of Lindisfarne, now Holy Island, as his base. Northumbria was already the strongest of the English kingdoms, and Aidan's own missionary work tied in well with a movement towards Christianity in other areas under Anglo-Saxon rule. In 597 a continental mission found a base in the kingdom of Kent, whose queen was a Frankish Christian. Much of what is known about the English kingdoms comes from the work of Bede, and includes his account of what he saw as a defining movement towards unity, the Synod of Whitby in 664. In addition, a number of Gospel books, including the *Lindisfarne Gospels*, were produced in Northumbria which also acquired a local saint in the early period in Cuthbert, a monk of Lindisfarne.

The societies into which Christianity penetrated need to be considered if we are to understand how it developed. Ireland was, to use the phrase of the Irish historian D. A. Binchy, tribal, rural, hierarchical and familiar (Dillon 1954, 53-4, Meek 2000, 149). Ireland was a slave-owning society and one in which the position of women was very much second place. Personal identity was understood in relation to the family, in particular the *derbfine*, those descended in the male line from a common great-grandfather. This group had the responsibility for land-ownership, legal and military duties and the conduct of its members. Anglo-Saxon society, with a different language and law-code was also intensely hierarchical, slave-owning and the majority of young men were culled in early life (Cavill 1999). In the absence of towns, monasteries in Ireland came to provide for the safe-keeping of treasures, especially during strife. Irish society also had separate intellectual and craft-worker classes that produced oral poetry, and luxury items for church and court.

Although the belief and practice of Irish, Welsh and later Anglo-Saxon Christianity was orthodox, it had some distinguishing features. One was the unusual degree to which it was organised around monasticism, although diocesan structures existed. In some cases double monasteries developed, probably from women's foundations which required priestly services. The two best-known, Kildare in Ireland (which eventually became a women-only establishment) and Whitby on the north-eastern English coast, were ruled by abbesses. Various local practices grew up, including the use in Ireland of an obscure form of learned Greek. Over the centuries there were liturgical developments which may have in some places included the use of the vernacular, the local language. The Irish seem also to have developed the practice of private confession of sins, and related to this, is the concept of *anam-chara*, soul friend, a person to whom one can tell their difficulties in the spiritual life. The penitential tradition was highly developed by the seventh century and long lists of penances for sins have survived. The monastic tradition also recognised a form of martyrdom, of leaving the known world and kinsfolk, to settle in a monastery in another territory where one's status would not be regarded, and possibly on an isolated island. This form of martyrdom could replace one not readily available locally, of shedding one's blood for Christ. Finally, in certain areas regarding the calendar, the churches on the fringe of Europe fell behind continental practice, a matter that was normalised at different times in their history.

A Celtic church?

There was some adaptation to local social organisation and tradition, but the churches saw themselves as part of the universal church, in union with Rome, and they had regular contact with the wider church of the continent. Changes occurred over the long time-span usually associated with Celtic Christianity (O'Loughlin 2000b, 32), but belief and practice remained orthodox through the many centuries before the arrival of the

Normans on either island, and indeed may have increased as sea-travel improved. While many contemporary writers would see something distinctively separate about the Celtic and English churches, and certain figures, including the fifth century British monk Pelagius and ninth century John Scotus Eriugena, are given a high status, for example by Helen Julian (2004), Ian Bradley (1993, 62-9), Esther de Waal (1988, 75), and Philip Newell (1997, 8-38), we have to consider whether they were actually as significant to the Christian communities of the time. We may be attempting to make historically credible what we wish to believe.

This brings us to the concept of a 'Celtic Church', which is often used in juxtaposition to the 'Romanising (or Roman) Church'. This term came into use with the nineteenth century Breton Celticist Ernest Renan (1823-92), was adopted at the time when Celtic Studies were becoming a university subject, and remained into the mid-twentieth century in the works of academics, including the early Irish monastic scholar Kathleen Hughes. The term 'Celtic Church' usually served as shorthand for the organisational development of early church life, and in particular the role of the monasteries. It was extended by some scholars to cover other aspects, including forms of eremitical life, traditions of learning and penitential practice. The scholars who used did not intend to imply that there was an independent type of Christianity.

However, Protestant polemicists since the Reformation have sought evidence of a different church not bound to Rome, and so the term came to be used in a wider sense. While the polemics have become much modified, the term 'Celtic Church' is no longer used by academics but has recently been regarded as a separate form of Christianity, close to its perceived native roots. It is used to include both the early church in the areas of Celtic language and culture, and also Christianised England, in particular the church in the powerful Saxon kingdom of Northumbria. This is understandable, and touches on the origins, to be discussed in the next chapter, of the current movement. As Christina Harrington has pointed out in her 2002 book, academic works since the 1930s have become increasingly inaccessible to the general reader and most contemporary writers on Celtic spirituality are dependent on out-of-date scholarship.

While there are strong academic reasons to avoid terms such as 'Celtic Church', 'Celtic' culture, 'Celtic' art, 'Celtic' peoples and 'Celtic spirituality', to say nothing of 'Celtic' designs and 'Celtic' liturgies, there is a general agreement that there are defining concepts that went beyond the language groups and legal systems. Some aspects are distinctive though not unique to Christianity in these islands, and there was clearly considerable cultural contact between the Gaelic world and those areas of England christianised from Iona, as we know for example by the way in which the style of the early Gospel books have much in common. However the gospels were written in the universal church language, Latin, and art being visual can move across boundaries. We need also to consider the restrictions imposed by mutually unintelligible languages.

One consequence of the popularity of Celtic spirituality today has been that a number of modern academic translations, anthologies and commentaries on original material, have appeared. They include those we have already considered and also Gilbert Márkus and Thomas Clancy's edition of Iona poetry (1995), Oliver Davies and Fiona Bowie's anthology of Welsh material (1995) and John Carey's selection of early Irish material (2000). Whether they will feed into, and moderate, the popular understanding of Celtic Christianity, remains to be seen.

Celtic Christianity and Celtic Twilights

We have already considered the basic elements of Celtic Christianity, and will now look in more detail at what is considered to be 'Celtic' and the ways in which there have been periods when the 'Celtic' has influenced religious belief and practice.

The first period of influence involved founders of monasteries and missionaries to non-Christian areas of Europe in the early middle ages, a period often described as the Age of the Saints. There was certainly an exchange of scholarship and books, especially Gospel books, the materials and artistic models for making new books and other church essentials, from which Britain and Ireland both gained, while an increase in scholarship must have had reciprocal advantages. We are also fortunate in that some of the best-loved early texts in both Latin and Irish have been preserved at monasteries aboard. There is also the question of

whether any distinctive practices or beliefs from the Celtic or
Anglo-Saxon worlds influenced wider European culture. There
is an ongoing debate about the influence, and indeed the beliefs,
of Pelagius, a monk thought to be from Britain, whose views
were condemned as heresy but which have sparked new discussion; and a renewed interest in the writings of the ninth-century
philosopher John Scotus Eriugena.

While we know relatively little about whether the countries
on the edge of Europe had much influence in the early medieval
period, we know considerably more about the explosion of literature in the twelfth century and later when stories from the
Celtic world, both secular and religious, became very popular.
This has been noted in relation to the movement by Ian Bradley
(1999, 39-76) and more extensively by Donald Meek (2000), but
it is worth looking at it in more detail because of the effect it still
has on our expectations of what is Celtic.

From the publication in the early twelfth century of the
Breton *lais* of Marie de France, Celtic tales became popular far beyond the lands where these languages were spoken. Works that
to a modern mind are more obviously religious, such as the voyage of Saint Brendan, passed in Latin across Europe and were
translated into many languages. Less read today but immensely
popular in their own time were the Visions of Tundale and of the
Knight Owen at the island in Lough Derg which is still a place of
rigorous penitential pilgrimage. Feeding into the insular practice
of pilgrimage, these stories took them to new heights, expanding
the readers' imaginations, in the case of Brendan to beyond the
shores of the known world, and in the case of Tundale and Owen
to realms beyond death. There are also the Arthurian cycle of
legends, which contain many apparent borrowings from Celtic
wonder-tale, and which have been provided with an ethical and
religious context. The impact of medieval stories can be considered as part of the background to our own form of Celtic spirituality as their influence can be seen in the mid-twentieth-century
works of J. R. R. Tolkien and C. S. Lewis. They have given us
something of the belief that Celts were, and are, wild, untamed,
adventurous, and endlessly in pursuit of the spiritual.

Donald Meek, and following him his former colleague Ian
Bradley, who specialises in nineteenth-century Scottish hymnody

but also writes on Celtic spirituality, charted other key times and places in which the 'Celtic' has been put to religious use in ways that still have an impact today. Significant for the development of the current movement is the way in which 'Celtic' themes came to the fore during the religious upheavals of the sixteenth and seventeenth centuries (Meek 2000, 110-18, 213-30).

Meek shows how the Reformed traditions created their own versions of the Celtic past to provide a sense of continuity in faith, and how these theories were later adapted to suit different denominational requirements. In brief, the Reformed tradition of the sixteenth century set store on an early 'Celtic Church', which was becoming increasingly known as the writings of church historians and antiquarians became available to a wider public through the printed word. They depicted it as pure, gospel-orientated and distinct from the Roman Church until overrun and corrupted by it. Saint Columba and others were presented as having brought an unsullied faith to the Scots, and there was good reason to reclaim this true form of Christianity for the people, which had first been received not in Latin but in the people's own tongue.

Meanwhile, the Catholic Irish and their descendants in Scotland have argued for the continuity between the church of Columba and their own persecuted one. Both traditions regarded as theirs the earliest Christianity in these islands, though modern ecumenical sensibilities mean that, even where still believed, this is rarely stated in public today. When Celtic Christianity developed in the 1980s in northern England, it was portrayed as a recovery of an original native Christianity common to both islands, a tool again for evangelism, one that was older than all denominational boundaries and belonged to everyone.

These approaches have stayed with us and explain why we expect a strong religious element in our understanding of the Celtic, even where we no longer agree with, or are interested in, the conflicts which led to different religious groupings 'claiming' the 'Celtic church' for their own.

The Reformation writers and their successors were followed by writers who took a literary approach that has also helped to form our contemporary expectations. The notion of the Celt as the mournful, misty, second-sighted character, forever looking back to a heroic past owes much to the immensely popular writing of James McPherson (1736-96), who presented supposedly ancient Gaelic myths preserved in poetic form to the public in 1760-65. While not specifically religious, they greatly influenced the late eighteenth-century Romantic Movement. At this period, too, a number of religious tourists visited Iona and its monastery, which was by then romantically ruinous, though accommodation on the island was less romantic, a matter commented upon in 1773 by Samuel Johnson who reached the island during his tour with James Boswell of the Hebrides (MacArthur 1991, 15-16, Power 2006, 38). Most tourists, however, saw what they hoped to see. The youthful composer Mendelssohn described wild islands, the basalt pillars of Staffa and the ruins on Iona, but not the indigenous population's poverty, or their attempts to farm, fish, cope with tourism and stay on land that was being turned over to sheep.

Another eighteenth-century influence was the Welshman, Iolo Morganwg (Edward Williams, 1747-1826), who attributed poems he published in 1789 to the fourteenth-century poet of love and the natural world, Dafydd ap Gwilym, and followed this by publishing other, allegedly druid, works. Iolo Morganwg's influence continues into the present within the neo-Pagan movements, especially in relation to his depictions of the druids, who are the subject of a recent book by the historian Ronald Hutton (*The Druids*, 2007).

Iolo Morganwyg's presentation of the Celt as an impractical dreamer who was the repository of ancient lore and a true spirituality came with its contrasting image, that of the pragmatic Saxon who was developing the mechanical skills of the Industrial Revolution. This juxtaposition may lie in part behind the interest in the 'Celtic' in the 1980s as traditional industries came to an end and the environmental impact started to be assessed.

Writers from previous ages have thus provided the background for our perceptions of Celtic spirituality, even when their works were not explicitly religious. Another development, which has had direct impact on current views, occurred towards the end of the nineteenth century when, with the growth of the academic discipline of Celtic Studies, more and more early texts were printed, and became known to writers, artists and directly or indirectly to the general public. As many of the texts and commentaries published at the time are still influential, we need to look at how this occurred.

As we have seen, the term 'Celtic Church' was coined by the Breton scholar Ernest Renan in the mid-nineteenth century. His main field of study was philology, the study of language, but he had a Catholic theological training and took a profound interest in the spiritual nature of existence. His view of the Celts as shy, sensitive, artistic and deeply spiritual, pushed back to the edge of Europe, preserving a heritage of imagination and sadness in their poetry, custodians of the tales of past grandeur, and while geographically and culturally peripheral retaining a pure religion, is one with which many modern readers would resonate. Renan's approach and his impact on academics has been considered in depth by Donald Meek (2000, 45-53). It had a widespread impact in its own time, and another, artistic term emerged to complement Renan's Celtic Church.

The term 'Celtic Twilight' appeared in the closing decade of the nineteenth century, when a collection of supernatural writings by William Butler Yeats was published under this name in 1893. The term was used to refer to the Irish Literary Revival of about 1890 to 1920, a movement which also saw the birth of an Irish national theatre and an outpouring of artistic activity. In Ireland the Revival had strong links with nationalistic politics, while the artistic side of the movement was paralleled in Scotland by the Celtic Revival. This period in both countries has had a profound impact on the understanding of the Celtic, which in turn was to influence the next and much more consciously spiritual Twilight *fin-de-siècle*, of the late twentieth century.

Lit by the Celtic Twilight – works behind the modern movement
The Celtic Twilight has left many works both of literature and art that retain their influence today. The one that has most inspired current writers came out of Gaelic Scotland and was a product of the nineteenth-century practice, found across Europe, of collecting folk tradition.

Carmichael's six-volume *Carmina Gadelica*, a compendium of poems, prayers and other verse in Gaelic, comes from material collected in the Hebrides, much of it in Catholic South Uist, at the close of the nineteenth century, and is accompanied by his English translations. Carmichael was a Gaelic-speaking Protestant, who combined his professional work as an Exciseman with a love of tradition and, unusually, collected as much from women as men, a feature that gives a breadth to his material that is not often found in collections of the time. He published at first in journals, and the first two volumes of the full collection appeared in his lifetime. Three more were edited by family members and the final volume was produced by the scholar and tradition-bearer Angus Matheson. The volumes were republished sporadically by the Scottish Academic Press, and were relatively little known outside academe until the 1980s.

The *Carmina Gadelica* is a collection of great beauty and its moving nature was apparent when translations of the religious material were printed for a wider audience. A small collection of the English translations was published in 1960 as *The Sun Dances* and G. R. D. MacLean's versified forms of some of the prayers, *Poems of the Western Highlanders*, appeared in 1961. A similar collection by Alastair McLean, *Hebridean Altars* had been published in 1937 (reprinted 1988) and they were supplemented in 1975 by a collection of writings by a Scottish Episcopalian priest and hermit Martin Reith, *God in our midst*. Once the movement had taken off these books became much in demand. *The Sun Dances* was repeatedly reprinted, another small, easily-handled collection, *New Moon of the Seasons*, appeared in 1986 and was reprinted in 1992, while in 1992 the English translations of the entire *Carmina Gadelica* were reprinted in paperback.

There has been some question over the extent to which Carmichael can be considered reliable, and whether his work genuinely reflects what was recounted by bearers of the oral tradition. A number of other collectors were working at the same time as Carmichael, and the formal standards that are now expected were only just developing. Unlike another collector of verse, the American Francis John Child, whose *English and Scottish Popular Ballads* remains the standard work in the field, Carmichael did not collect music, and it is assumed that the prayers did not have melodies assigned to them but were said privately. Also unlike Child, Carmichael did not classify and print side-by-side different variants. He sometimes appears to have silently combined two or more pieces which he believed to be parts of the same prayer. However, his material is not unlike what is found in Irish collections of the same period. His methods of collecting, at a time before sound recording was possible, would have required him to write down rapidly what he had heard, especially if he was receiving personal prayers from people not used to the kind of public performance normal for traditional storytelling or singing. It is possible too that Carmichael saw himself as the last of a line of tradition-bearers, and if so, he may have seen himself as doing in print what many tradition-bearers may also do. In fact, silently joining one or more versions may be more common where a prayer, or charm or poem is intended for personal use than in a public recitation of well-known stories from the traditional repertoire. Carmichael may also have decided not to adopt the developing collecting conventions because he saw himself as dealing with the stuff of people's souls, and as recording a different class of material to the stories and songs that occupied people's hours of entertainment. His sources were possibly more fluid and individual, and less susceptible to the rigorous process a collector could adopt with a locally well-known singer or storyteller, who would have been aware of the significance of their repertoire and the need to record it correctly. If Carmichael indeed cut or joined, he did it with a sensitivity to language and culture.

Whether his collection is a totally authentic portrayal of Hebridean spirituality may be under some doubt, but it has been crucial in the growth of modern Celtic spirituality, and the contents are often cited, especially the prayers that have three-fold invocations, or concern everyday activities of the time, such as household or farming tasks, or concern the natural world, travel or the seasons. Their immediacy and use of vivid descriptive terms means that recent writers have attributed an intimacy and immediacy in the Hebrideans' relationship with God, a sense of God present in the everyday activities of life and in the turn of the seasons, and a firm belief that God is protecting them and holding them in community. Almost nothing, however, is known of whether these publications circulated among Highlands and Islands churchgoers, whether in Gaelic or English, and, if they were, what was made by the Protestant majority of what is

predominantly Catholic material, including prayers addressed
to the Virgin Mary, the archangel Michael and Saints Columba
and Brigit, to say nothing of the charms, auguries, heroic chants
and other material that the *Carmina Gadelica* contains.

It is known that Carmichael's translations began to have a
substantial impact in the later 1970s and early 1980s on English-
language writers like David Adam and the compilers of the Iona
liturgies. While the themes and content will be considered later,
it is also interesting to see how the form of these prayers was
copied. Many of those by David Adam contain a threefold invocation. Many of Carmichael's prayers had strong regular rhythms
associated with waulking cloth or rowing a boat, and many end
with a repeated line. Similar features are used to give the distinctive 'Celtic' taste to contemporary works in English.

Another way in which they were emulated was in their language. Carmichael had made attempts to render into English the
Gaelic cadences and phraseology. His translations often use the
present continuous verbal form, 'I am bending my knees / in the
eye of the Father who created me ...', a form which is common
in Gaelic but where in English the simple present, 'I bend', is
normal. He also gave equivalents in English for the verbal prepos-
itions that carry specific meaning in Gaelic. Consequently, forms
like 'Bless to me ...' have become an easily recognisable feature
of the prayers of current Celtic spirituality. What have been
portrayed as examples of the poetic nature of the Gael, and relished for their combination of strangeness and comprehensibility,
is a nineteenth-century stylistic quirk, an attempt to reproduce
something of the original language. Carmichael's may be more
valid than the pseudo-archaisms of many nineteenth-century
literary works, but they belong to the culture of their period
rather than to anything quintessentially Gaelic.

A number of other works from the last Celtic Twilight also
influenced the development of Celtic spirituality. Under the
name Fiona MacLeod appeared works by the lyrical writer, critic,
partial Gaelic-speaker and Celtic revivalist William Sharp (1855-
1905). His prolific writing career was pursued under numerous
pen-names, and in the early 1880s he edited and wrote most of
the short-lived *Pagan Review*. A member of the esoteric Order of
the Golden Dawn he was in touch with many of the leaders of

the Celtic movement of the time, including the Irish poet W. B. Yeats. He spent his later years largely on Iona, and his books published by his widow after his death, *From the Hills of Dream* (1910) and *Iona* (1910), were sympathetic to Christianity, if unorthodox, for example in their views on the femininity of God and a Second Coming at which Christ would return in female form. Sharp's main influence on the contemporary Celtic movement is that his style was imitated and his poems used by George MacLeod and other members of the Iona Community in the 1950s and 1960s. *Iona* and extracts from it were reprinted throughout the twentieth century.

One character who is rarely or never mentioned but who may have had considerable influence in the background is a younger contemporary of Carmichael's, Marjorie Kennedy-Fraser (1857-1930). A singer of Scots Gaelic extraction, she collected songs in Gaelic direct from traditional singers when they would otherwise have been lost, and ahead of her time, she used a phonograph and wax cylinders to record them. With her translator, Kenneth Macleod, she produced three volumes between 1909 and 1921, with a fourth volume following some years later. She adapted Hebridean songs for the drawing-room, and the music and, even more, her texts often have little to do with the originals. However, she made no secret of how she intended to treat her collection, left notes about her sources, and retained the original recordings, which were later given to the University of Edinburgh. She is regarded with ambiguity by modern traditional singers, most of whom have less affinity with the contemporary Celtic movement than she had with the people she collected. Her ashes were buried on Iona, which she often visited towards the end of her life.

In Ireland, Douglas Hyde produced a work similar to the religious sections of Carmichael's collection. *The Religious Songs of Connacht* (1906) in turn encouraged others to collect more folk material, much of it religious, in the Irish language. This impetus continued throughout the twentieth century, and provided many of the prayers in Irish that are used today. One in particular, *Ag Críost an síol*, 'To Christ the seed', or 'Christ's is the seed', is widely known in the setting by the composer Seán Ó Riada (1931-71).

Ireland is the focus but specific attention is paid to Brittany in the Benedictine monk Louis Gougaud's monumental study of the early Middle Ages, originally published as *Les Chrétientés celtiques* (1911) but better known through the revised and much extended English version, published in 1932 as *Christianity in Celtic Lands*. This owes much to the Old Irish scholar Maud Joynt, who is modestly credited as the translator. It has contributed to the more scholarly end of the current movement, has been reprinted, and while very dated, is useful as a comprehensive survey of early Irish and other Celtic church history and culture.

A key literary contribution was made by the German scholar Kuno Meyer (1858-1919) who produced translations into English from Old Irish as *Selections from Early Irish Poetry* in 1911. This book may have been forgotten outside academe but that it contained his English translation of Saint Patrick's Breastplate. It was not the first translation – Cecil Frances Alexander's hymn 'I bind unto myself today' was based on an earlier version – but while retranslations have been attempted, Meyer's remains the best-known. Meyer was much influenced by the Celtic Twilight and has been criticised in recent times for his overtly romantic attitude to the poetry, and to his claims for the nature poetry as innately Celtic, a theme that as we have seen is central in the current movement. Meek (2000, 50-54) has shown how a rigorous scholar like Meyer could also, like Renan, extend the concept of the Celtic beyond linguistics to accommodate the Celtic Twilight. A good poet in a language not his own, his main purpose was to make accessible the poetry of early Ireland, and he includes a fair amount of religious poetry, some but not all of which has found favour with the movement. Meyer prints for example the macaronic, part-Latin, part-Irish, eleventh-century hymn 'Deus Meus, adiuva me', sometimes sung in Irish-language religious services; and the poem, 'The hermit', which is rarely quoted in his translation, but in other versions has influenced recent writers.

Meyer's student and contemporary Eleanor Hull (1860-1935) produced her *Poem-book of the Gael* in 1913. She like Meyer printed 'Deus Meus, adiuva me' and 'The Hermit', but is best known today for her versification of the translation by Mary Byrne

(1880-1931) of an early Irish poem, 'Be thou my vision'. This hymn has become popular in England only in recent decades, possibly because it was widely used in cross-community services broadcast from the north of Ireland during the Troubles. Hull and Byrne belonged to the first generation of women scholars, an achievement that is rarely acknowledged by those who use their works today, even though the current movement makes high claims for the status of women in the early 'Celtic Church'.

Much of the motivation for the Celtic Twilight petered out after the First World War and the independence of most of Ireland, but some works in similar vein to those we have considered were published throughout the twentieth century. In Ireland, the anthologies of the academics Meyer and Hull were followed by those of others, who produced them for small audiences, largely comprised of students, but who intended their works for the general reader as well. The first of these, Gerard Murphy's *Early Irish lyrics, eighth to twelfth century*, printed in 1956, gives the Irish verse with parallel prose translations. This collection has not been republished and seems to be little known directly, but other writers have versified several of his translations. Some of these in turn are found in contemporary works on Celtic spirituality, especially poems of exile attributed to Saint Columba, which are used in connection with the theme of pilgrimage.

Two other collections circulated mainly within academic circles until the movement took off in the 1980s, when their contents became more widely known. *A Golden Treasury of Irish poetry AD 600-1200*, edited with translations by David Greene and Frank O'Connor, first appeared in 1967. Again the translations are in prose and follow the originals closely, but this collection has enjoyed more favour than Murphy's and has recently been reissued. As with *Early Irish Lyrics*, not all the material is religious and that which is religious has not all been accepted by the movement, most notably the poems pertaining to the Virgin Mary. O'Connor was a recognised poet who made a number of other translations from early Irish poetry, secular as well as sacred. His verse translations, scattered through other anthologies, are far better known than his contributions to this scholarly work.

Also first published in 1967 was James Carney's *Medieval Irish Lyrics* which contains poems from a slightly later period than

Murphy's *Early Irish Lyrics*. The medieval feel of these poems may make them more accessible to the general public than the earlier Irish poetry, and the parallel translations are given in verse. These considerations that may have led to this volume's wider usage and earlier reprinting. However, the publishers, aiming at a student rather than a 'Celtic spirituality' market, incorporated into the 1985 reprinting another short work of Carney's, *The Irish Bardic Poet*, which is unlikely to be of interest from the perspective of spirituality.

These anthologies, which were subsidised by the Irish State because of their Irish language content, had short print-runs, and it is only recently that they have become easily available again. This may be partly due to the Celtic Christianity movement but also to do with the increasing number of people interested in studying Ireland's cultural heritage.

The official promotion of the Irish language led to the circulation of a number of works with an even narrower audience. Drawing upon genuine tradition are the publications of three Catholic priests, Diarmuid Ó Laoghaire (1982, 1989), Pádraig Ó Fiannachta (Ó Fiannachta and Forristal 1988), and Seán Ó Duinn (1984, 1990). Ó Laoghaire took folk prayers from existing collections or short-lived journals, and from the *Carmina Gadelica* (silently translating Scots Gaelic into Irish), with the intention of making them accessible to Irish-speakers for personal and family devotion. Ó Fiannachta published similar traditional material with parallel English translations by Forristal. Ó Duinn created liturgies in Irish for domestic as well as church use from traditional material (1984), wrote in Irish on the folk tradition of Ireland, Scotland and Wales (1990), and later published in English on Celtic spirituality for a wider audience (2000). These writers have fed into the Irish version of modern Celtic spirituality, but their original purpose was to keep the Irish language alive and its users nourished. Only Ó Duinn in his most recent work consciously contributed to the current movement.

Recently, a collection intended for modern Irish devotional use has been compiled by Donla Uí Bhraonáin (2008). This contains prayers in Irish with accompanying English translations, derived from Ó Laoghaire, Douglas Hyde, and previously unpublished folk prayers. A few of the prayers she has used from

Ó Laoghaire's collection are originally from the Scots Gaelic *Carmina Gadelica*.

The writers used genuine traditional prayers, most of which had been printed but which are very similar to unpublished material, the majority of it in Irish, to be found in the national collection of Irish folklore begun in 1927 and now housed at University College Dublin. This collection had been mocked in its time, for example by the satirist Myles na gCopaleen (Brian O'Nolan, better known as Flann O'Brien) who memorably described it as containing 'twenty tons of Irish folklore', but is a substantial repository for those seeking to develop an authentic Celtic spirituality by using the beliefs and practices, and the religious stories told by the 'common people', and at least one other recent writer has used it (Clancy 1999). Meanwhile, liturgical experiments using traditional themes but in English have also been attempted by another Irish writer, Brendan O'Malley (1998).

Other literature, religious and otherwise, from all the Celtic-speaking regions was published in accessible form during the early-to-mid-twentieth century. The most notable collections were by Kenneth Jackson, whose first anthology was a scholarly one, published in 1935, but he went on to produce *A Celtic Miscellany* for a popular readership in 1951. Revised and published in the Penguin Classic series in 1971, this contains translations of verse and prose works in all six Celtic languages; covers the period from the earliest vernacular works in the eighth century to oral and written traditions of the nineteenth century; remains the most comprehensive introduction in English to the subject; is well-annotated; cheap and always in print. While now dated, and arguably subject to the same romantic approaches in particular to the nature poetry as Meyer and Hull have been criticised for, it gives a valuable overview of Celtic literature, and provides the necessary context in which to understand the specifically religious elements. However, in spite of these advantages, it is relatively little cited in recent popular books.

While only a small proportion of people in twentieth-century Ireland use Irish on a daily basis, the more widespread use of the Welsh language means that collections, many of them bilingual, are known to those who used Welsh as their language of worship. While most of the users are unlikely to regard themselves as associated with the current movement, or willing to accept its tenets, during the 1980s modern Celtic spirituality benefited from their traditions. One of the earliest proponents, A. M. Allchin, had learned Welsh, and was thus able to introduce an element of reality regarding the culture, and prayers taken from Welsh, into the movement.

More controversially, the poems of R. S. Thomas (1913-2000), most of which are in English, are found in many anthologies of contemporary Celtic Christianity. He is no doubt included primarily because of the quality of his poems, but because he was Welsh and wrote about the natural world, he is frequently regarded, though he may not have wished it, as part of a continuing Celtic tradition.

Though rarely credited as providing sources for the movement, Helen Waddell (1889-1965) may have been indirectly influential. *The Wandering Scholars* was published in 1927 for a popular audience but contained the results of much learning. She drew references not only from own her field of study, European poetry in Latin from the early Christian 'Dark Ages', but included comparisons with the poetry of later authors and even some by her own contemporaries. She was writing *belles lettres*, not direct scholarship, and her methods were similar to the methods of many recent writers on Celtic spirituality. Her *Medieval Latin Lyrics* (1929) is a collection of translations which has considerable potential for the future development of the 'Celtic' movement, but her *Beasts and Saints* (1934), a retelling of traditional tales of the saints, has been the most used, though her authorship is not always acknowledged. The first section contains stories about the Desert Fathers, while the second contains English and Irish saints' tales, including frequently-cited stories of Saints Columba and a crane, Columba and a white horse, Kevin and a blackbird, Cuthbert and ravens, Cuthbert and otters, and legends of Saint Brendan.

Waddell was, like Hyde and Hull, an Irish Protestant, and though in her case she was from the north, it may be significant how much the minority religious communities have contributed to the development of our knowledge of Celtic spirituality. She was also a member of another minority group we have already mentioned, the women scholars and poets who, together with others, have made the ancient poetry accessible to us.

The works we have considered, and others of their kind, set the scene for the development of the Celtic movement in the 1980s. While they were available to those interested in the literature and poetry of the 'Celtic fringe', they had not been produced for a specifically religious market, and many of the new writers on Celtic spirituality express their delight in having stumbled upon them. Nor were they then used systematically, for different writers knew different works, and most concentrated on just one of the Celtic countries. They mined the material for devotional purposes, had limited knowledge of the historical and cultural contexts in which the works were produced, and what they did know was often from works of outdated scholarship. What is more, they worked more or less independently of each other, and they probably did not intend to create a Celtic movement. Their aims were to present to a wider audience material which had moved them and which seemed to be relevant to contemporary spiritual concerns. We now turn to what happened at that period.

CHAPTER THREE

The Twentieth-century Twilight:
Texts for a new age

We have seen that the later twentieth-century Celtic movement relied heavily on translations into English by scholars who were writing either for an academic or for a popular Irish or Scottish audience. They were not aware that their works would be used by an unexpected audience, in particular in England, to develop what is now known as Celtic spirituality, and that the material and the themes would be taken up by writers and retreat-givers.

The current movement's emphasis is on the written, translated, word, and the sources we considered in the last chapter were used by the initial writers of the 1980s, many of whom also produced their adaptations, meditations and poetic reflections. While this was a natural development, writers who came to the movement later did not distinguish between the traditional sources and these new artistic creations. They often generated their own works based on these publications, without distinguishing between what was ancient or traditional, perhaps unaware of how much was the interpretation or creation of the recent writer. We therefore need to look briefly at what the first writers of the 1970s and 1980s produced, and their church, society and cultural background, and then to explore some of the themes that have developed, and their continuing attraction.

The movement which took off with such rapidity in the 1980s owes much to the writer and university lecturer Esther de Waal, who had already made a name popularising Benedictine spirituality. She and Donald Allchin produced *Threshold of Light* (1986), a collection of Welsh and Gaelic poetry for devotional use. De Waal's *The Celtic Vision* (1988) is a collection of the English texts of the religious poems from Carmichael's *Carmina Gadelica*. Her companion work, *A World made Whole* (1991) is her description of the 'Celtic' spiritual world, which she draws from ancient poetry and relatively modern folk tradition. At the same time other writers, in particular David Adam, were mining the same sources as hers, also for spiritual purposes.

The wonder these writers expressed in finding works of Celtic literature and folk tradition is infectious, and they did great service by making them easily available to others. They did not approach their sources systematically, and unintentionally developed an aspect of the movement which exasperates many of its critics, its eclecticism. The writers wanted people to know beautiful works, whether from the seventh or nineteenth centuries, and saw no difficulty in including these side-by-side. By doing this they went beyond accepted academic boundaries, though what they did was not greatly different from that of compilers of many anthologies. Indeed, one of the aspects of the material that entranced them was what they saw it as all-encompassing, able to cover every aspect of life. Their writings reflect something of this all-encompassing perspective in the way they included everything and were happy to move between periods, languages and works produced for differing purposes. These writers and others who followed them saw the poems of the *Carmina Gadelica* as continuing a tradition formed by early Irish and medieval Welsh nature poets and, because the works were available in English, treated them as part of the common heritage of these islands. They saw no difficulty in combining Gaelic folk poetry with selections from Anglo-Saxon literature, or texts written in Latin. The focus was specifically spiritual and the material harvested was seen as all relating to God and being relevant to the search for the divine in contemporary society. In consequence, a combination that had worked for the individual could be expected to speak to a wider audience. If reinterpretation was deemed necessary, it was provided. De Waal, for example, who produced several books on Celtic spirituality, then reproduced Waddell's *Beasts and Saints* in a form she saw as suitable for a late-twentieth-century audience (Waddell 1995).

This contemporary movement makes little distinction between recently-composed personal contributions and original texts, some of them centuries old, treating them all as part of a continuum. Contemporary writers feel free to add to what they see as the tradition modern poems that appeal to them, and also ones they have composed themselves. Devotional works by writers like

David Adam and members of the Northumbria Community include poems, prayers and reflections that have worked in some context liturgically. The all-embracing nature of Celtic Christianity has developed, at least in part, because the term is used to embrace so much.

While the all-embracing approach further ensures that what comprises Celtic spirituality is not always clear, it is certainly a movement that sees organised Christianity as monolithic and excessively masculine, even when the intention of the writers is to reform it or make Christian faith more accessible. Books, poems and artistic works from the last Celtic Revival, Celtic music, in particular in its gentler instrumental forms, and dance as a form of self-expression, are all used.

There is also a key feature which differentiates the current movement from previous Celtic Twilights. This is the absence of gloom. There is neither the contrived yearning for a golden age long gone as in the last Celtic Twilight, nor is there the extensive sense of guilt that pervaded both traditional Calvinistic Presbyterianism and, until recently, Roman Catholicism. This is a happy movement in which the 'Celtic' is regarded as good and wholesome, and will at last overcome the dominance of the miserable and churchy, an understanding that inevitably influences the selection of themes and texts.

Motivations and movements

Meek (2000, 23-30) gave a summary of what he considers the most significant cultural factors in the development of Celtic Christianity in Britain since the 1960s. He includes the reaction against orthodoxy and dogmatism in society in general, against the materialistic politics of the Thatcher period in Britain, the concern for the environment, the decline in church attendance, and a desire to connect with native roots. He notes that other countries have similar movements drawing upon their indigenous spiritualities, in particular in North America, and many writers draw conscious parallels with the Celtic. This continent has been particularly susceptible to Celtic spirituality because of the numbers of people who trace the ancestry to Ireland (2000, 17-18).

Another major influence may be traced to the influence across western Christianity of the Second Vatican Council in the early 1960s. Within the Roman Catholic Church, the use of the vernacular language for liturgy, greater participation by lay people, and a move away from rigid rules to more spontaneous expressions of faith with greater emphasis on the worshipping community, all prepared the ground for the reception of Celtic Christianity, and the use of prayers, music and sometimes dance 'in the Celtic tradition' into church services.

There was a corresponding move in Catholic spirituality to a more intensive concentration on the individual and their personal spiritual growth. One-to-one retreats, group retreats and themed events all flourished in retreat houses throughout Britain and Ireland. Many Catholics have moved away from traditional sacramental confession but it is increasingly common for them, and members of other churches who are seriously seeking to develop their faith, to have a spiritual director with whom to discuss aspects of their life. In particular Ignatian spirituality, based on a modern interpretation of the *Spiritual Exercises* of Ignatius Loyola, the founder of the Jesuits, became very popular in the 1980s. This approach, which emphasises the use of the imagination and the senses, and provides the opportunity to relate one's spiritual experience to a trained director, provided members of religious orders with new opportunities for personal development. Simplified and cheaper versions of the one-to-one retreat, including those taking part in the home, became available to laypeople. In turn, numerous people, especially women, have trained as spiritual directors and found a new role in church life.

Catholic Liturgy, and also the liturgies of other churches, were open to development in ways that may be regarded as 'Celtic'. The Roman Catholic Office of Morning and Evening Prayer produced in the 1970s, which is used by priests, members of religious orders and some laypeople, contains a number of hymns which are not otherwise generally known. Though unattributed, several of them are derived from collections of early Irish poetry, in particular those of Murphy (1956) and Carney (1967). Whether these have been recognised as 'Celtic' or not, they may have prepared the ground for a greater acceptance of the imagery. Certainly, prayers, poems and new liturgies in the 'Celtic tradition', whether they were indeed ancient or were modern derivatives, became commonplace at religious conferences, and the 'Celtic' gained credence as an alternative to traditional religious material.

Another feature, at least in the form to which Celtic spirituality has adapted in North America, was identified by Christina Harrington ((2001, 11) as the popularity of the writings of the American Matthew Fox, who is a proponent of what he has named Creation spirituality. His views are significant as they have parallels in the development of the movement in Europe and may have directly influenced it. Fox was a Dominican friar and a trained theologian when he published *Original Blessing* in 1983. Subtitled *A primer in creation spirituality*, this rapidly became widely known and caused great interest and also controversy, in particularly with the Vatican, a matter that may have increased its sales among western Catholics. In this book and at greater length in later works, he argues that the universe is basically a blessing, that humanity experiences it as naturally good, and that humans are naturally blessed rather than born in original sin. He believes the divine is both male and female, is present within all of us, is present in the world and is encountered by humans, though not exclusively, in and through the world. We have to dig within ourselves to find our true selves through experience of the spiritual. He relates his theology to native spiritualities in other cultures, including those of North America, saying that it is an ancient spirituality recovered rather than a new one. His books are aimed at a general audience, and seek to address issues in twentieth-century Christianity, in particular the recovery of joy.

His approach may have influenced proponents of the Celtic movement to varying degrees. Fox would be of little interest on the more evangelical end as Creation spirituality seems to diminish the unique qualities of Christianity, including its historical roots and understanding of the nature of Christ. At times, modern spiritualities of this kind may seem to merge with a general benign pantheism. On the other hand, the change of emphasis away from original sin to original blessing relates to what is understood of the Pelagian controversy, and as Pelagius appears to have come from Britain, his influence on a theology of original grace is thought to have been especially widespread on both islands until the Synod of Whitby. Consequently, his perceived theology is seen as part of the ancient and recoverable heritage of faith. Pelagius is known to have wished to instil in Christians a stronger sense of ethical responsibility for their actions, and his views have been interpreted as a belief that all humans are born with the grace needed, and that Christ gives them the choice between good and sin (Van de Weyer 190, 3, *Celtic Daily Prayer* 2005, 141-2). Though not always accepted as factual, for instance by Bradley (1999, 199, 231), this understanding is seen to assist people to see God as intimately involved with their lives and therefore that they can engage in life joyfully.

Another possible influence may be a general one derived from Fox's engagement with feminist spirituality and his appreciation of the equal role of women. His being censored by the Vatican may not have harmed his popular appeal, while his riposte to the then Cardinal Ratzinger and his leaving his religious order and the priesthood, may all have assisted with his image as a free spirit with a spontaneous awareness of the goodness in creation and a spirituality than cannot be controlled through lifeless church structures.

Fox is an example of a Catholic writer who influenced members of other denominations, while ecumenical developments permitted the wider sharing of material. Catholics as well as the original Presbyterian audiences began to use material produced by the Wild Goose Worship Group of the Iona Community. This corpus included modern hymns and liturgies which used traditional folk tunes and rhythmic prose that emulated the *Carmina Gadelica*. The words of the hymns were radical calls for justice, and emphasised Christian responses to poverty, to the treatment of the outsider, and to other uncomfortable facets of contemporary society. These themes may have been hard to digest, but the tunes were easy to sing and musically suitable for communal use, were sufficiently close to the folk tradition to be partially known, and were widely appreciated. So, under the umbrella of the Celtic movement, hymns and liturgies containing hard-hitting commentary on issues of social concern were acclaimed by audiences who may have had limited social engagement themselves.

Another factor in the development of the movement was that

in the late 1980s the evangelical wing of the Anglican Church and some Non-Conformists were preparing for a 'Decade of Evangelism'. This was intended as a national cross-denomin-ational movement to encourage people to come to church, and it inspired some of the books that presented the 'Celtic' as a tool for mission to the non-churchgoers in British society.

From another perspective entirely, these decades saw the growth of an environmental movement, a desire to live more lightly on the land, a movement which has had a profound effect in most Christian circles. The evidence for climate change in-creased and it was seen more and more as something caused by humans and to have the worst effects on the poor across the world. The spiritual responsibility for stewarding creation be-came a major theme in European Christianity, particularly among the majority with middle-class lifestyles and incomes. People supporting projects in developing countries heard at first hand of the detrimental effects of climate change and also of the need to take action in their own lives, at least to the extent of recycling and cutting back on waste, using fairly-traded and organically-produced food and cleaning products, and some-times to more radical and sacrificial changes of lifestyle. The nature poetry of early Christian Ireland and Wales and the sense of closeness to the natural world evident in the *Carmina Gadelica* were ideal resources for a socially responsible engage-ment with, and appreciation of, the created order. This concern was also found in another emerging area of spirituality to which we shall turn later, modern forms of paganism which emphasise a close affinity with the earth and with the seasons.

'Celtic' politics
We need also to consider the political and social context. The 1980s and early 1990s in Britain were a time of social change as a traditional industrial base gave way to a money economy, while unemployment increased, welfare benefits were cut, and the gap between rich and poor widened. Simultaneously, access by the middle classes to higher education increased, and women became increasingly prominent in the workplace. The 1980s are most remembered for the eleven years leadership of Margaret Thatcher, the prime minister who famously declared that there

was no such thing as society. A sense of unease developed about the gap between those who were doing well but had narrow horizons, and those on whom the limitations of poverty had been imposed. By the mid 1990s it appeared that something had gone badly wrong,

The unease was also felt in church life, and became public when, in the wake of riots, the Church of England's *Faith in the City* (1985) challenged government with regard to social deprivation in traditional urban areas. Against this backdrop, it may be worth considering whether one of the attractions of the new Celtic spirituality was as spiritual rebellion by socially concerned churchgoers in favour of a gentler, more inclusive society.

Another move was afoot to distance parts of the nation from the economics of the City and the dominating culture of economic endeavour and consumer success based in the south of England. In the case of Northumbria, there were additional strains, for it was felt that both urban and rural areas had been neglected by distant London. The dependence on coalmining and its related heavy industries meant that the miners' strike of 1984-5 had devastating consequences on the local economy. This was followed in 1992 with the announcement that the coal industry was to be de-nationalised and the majority of the pits closed. This had a profound effect on an area where it had provided both jobs for life for miners and a large number of ancillary workers and a strong social network. It encouraged the increasing desire for more local decision-making, and this in turn may have encouraged the desire to be regarded as 'Celtic' and 'different' like Scotland and Wales, both of which were moving towards their own governance.

Northumbria became identified as 'Celtic'. Its ancient sacred places, especially Holy Island, provided a focus, and Bede's stories and the Gaelic poems proved to be models for literary interpretation and new creativity. It became possible for practitioners to see their spirituality as concerned with healing and harmony, and a locally-focused Celtic Christianity developed. A number of men promoted the concept, among them the writer and then Vicar of Lindisfarne, David Adam, and the founders of both the Christian Northumbria Community and Community of Aidan and Hilda.

The Northumbrian focus helped to set the movement apart from mainstream English society, and it also helped to set it apart in another way. The writers of the movement, like the majority of people involved in church life in Britain during the 1980s made no connection with, and perceived no spiritual or political responsibility for, problems in one very inharmonious part of the Celtic world, the north of Ireland, which was suffering violent social conflict. It proved possible, while including occasional prayers for an end to conflict in Northern Ireland, to develop a concept of the Celtic which bypassed the more uncomfortable contemporary aspects of political and church life in favour of a reclaimed and unsullied ideal.

Recovering the rediscovered
While Irish and Welsh poetry and prose provided much of the material from which Celtic spirituality drew, the movement was originally English and it appears that the slightly later adoption of Celtic spirituality in the traditional Celtic heartlands was a reaction by local writers to the harvesting of 'their' heritage. Even where they shared the same concerns as the English writers, and although they were predominantly English-speaking, the Irish, Scottish and Welsh proponents seem to have viewed themselves as custodians of the literary and artistic sources. There appears to have been a degree of unease when books appeared in print that showed the unconscious selectivity of the English-based writers, which did not tally with local and national perceptions of their heritage. It appeared as a form of cultural consumerism, taking of some aspects of the culture and changing them to suit a new audience without regard to the wider context and of how the culture was honoured in the places from which it had originated, or the languages which had given it birth. In consequence, Celtic spirituality developed at least in part in these lands in order to claim back the native heritage.

Unconscious cultural consumerism may be a matter for others as well as the dominant English writers to consider. Some of the Irish-language writers we have mentioned regularly took poems from the *Carmina Gadelica*, and adapted them silently for an Irish audience. Diarmaid Ó Laoghaire makes it clear that to him the prayers were part of a cultural continuum (1989, 69), but this was not necessarily the opinion of contemporary Hebrideans, even of those from the Catholic Gaelic-speaking part of the culture. While Ó Laoghaire was a sensitive writer, he concentrated almost entirely on the Catholic tradition, and unusually gives a context in which the folk prayers might have developed. He suggests that their use of scripture and apparent Rule of Life was in response to limited opportunities for priestly ministry available in the Hebrides in the later nineteenth century (1989, 282, 297). He also provided brief notes of his sources, and there is certainly some historical justification to indicate that the same prayers could have been present in Irish and well as Scots Gaelic.

Compilers of anthologies aimed at a Celtic spirituality audience from English perspective were doing the same thing with translations from Gaelic, where the difference in culture and language is so much greater, and few readers are able to refer to the originals. In each case, members of the larger cultural group were not necessarily aware of the extent to which they were 'cherry-picking' what they wished to take from a smaller and more vulnerable culture without reference to context or local sensibilities, and so far only Meek (2000) has considered their actions from the perspective of a native speaker.

While the majority of the founders of the movement were Northumbrian men, a number of the writers from Ireland are female. One apparent attraction of the 'Celtic' is that it enables people to have roles outside the formal Catholic structures. The movement developed among women disillusioned with ecclesiastical systems in which they perceive themselves as having no role. This was at a time when women expected equality with men before the law, in the workplace and in social life, and the fact that they were denied it within their Church structures, caused particular offence. Celtic spirituality enabled the development of a different worldview which included an equal respect for women. Women denied the more established forms of church work developed new areas such as the increasingly popular but financially fragile retreat work and spiritual direction, and these gave them opportunity to incorporate the 'Celtic' in prayers and songs into liturgy, and indeed dance. While Anglican women began to be ordained priests and took on

parish roles during the 1990s, church structures remained dominated by men, and they too may have found Celtic spirituality
attractive as it seemed to provide alternative models.

A directly spiritual boost to the movement occurred in the
years leading to the anniversaries in 1997 of the death of Columba
of Iona and the arrival of the continental mission led by Augustine
of Canterbury. Special pilgrimages took place and new books
were written to mark the occasion, for example those by John
Finney (1996) and Johnston MacMaster (1997), who portrayed the
missions of the past as tools for contemporary evangelisation. The
ancient churches of these islands were perceived by these and
other writers as spiritually vigorous, harmonious, mission-orientated, and environmentally respectful, images which sat well with
the desire for church renewal in the new millennium.

Social change in the later 1990s on both islands included a
change of government in Britain, and an end to armed conflict in
Northern Ireland, and these may also have helped the millennium
boost. This ideal harmonious former age, to which we all wish
to return, sat well with contemporary concerns, in particular
about the environment.

Popular art

Another boost may have come from literature and the cinema, as
films based on two series of books with Celtic overtones were released in the late 1990s. Two mid-twentieth century writers who are
best known for their fantasy literature, the friends and also fellow-
academics C. S. Lewis and J. R. R. Tolkien, had a profound knowledge of the Celtic and Anglo-Saxons worlds. While this knowledge
is not directly invoked in their fantasy fiction for children and
adults, it is nevertheless present. C. S. Lewis draws in particular on
the medieval adaptations of Celtic wonder-tales, while Tolkien's fiction is based more directly on the early medieval sources, particularly on the Welsh. Both were committed Christians, something that
is more explicit in Lewis's works than in Tolkien's, and for both
their faith was a motivating force in their writing.

Through Lewis claimed to dislike allegory in any form, his
Chronicles of Narnia and some of his adult fiction, in particular
his science-fiction trilogy, are replete with it. Tolkien, in the
meantime, could be disparaging about Celtic mythology:

'Celtic'… is … a magic bag, into which anything may be put, and out of which almost anything can come … anything is possible in the fabulous Celtic twilight, which is not so much a twilight of the Gods as of reason (Tolkien 1963, 29-30).

Even if anything could be drawn and any surmises made, he loved medieval Welsh and created a fictional Elvish language from it.

Both he and Lewis became very popular, and their works would have been know to the majority of those creating Celtic Christianity. At the turn of the millennium they became known to a new audience through the cinema. Three films based on Tolkien's *Lord of the Rings* were released to instant acclaim, and were followed by a film adaptation of Lewis' *The Lion, the Witch and the Wardrobe*, one of the earlier *Chronicles of Narnia*. The extent to which these two writers familiarised people with Celtic ideas must remain tentative, but the fact that these books received a new lease of life from the screen may have contributed to the religious understanding of Celtic spirituality.

There are also a few modern authors who, while not writing for devotional purposes, have taken up Celtic themes in their novels. The most noticeable are Peter Tremayne, the pen-name of Peter Beresford-Ellis, and Melvyn Bragg. Beresford-Ellis, who has written widely on Celtic themes but not on spirituality as such, produced a series of books featuring Sister Fidelma, a widely-travelled seventh-century Irish monastic sleuth. Bragg's novel *Credo* is a lengthy account based on the life, mainly fictional in the absence of sources, on the Irish female saint Bega, who settled in Cumbria. Both adopt characteristics expected of a 'Celtic' work: a female protagonist; a gentle faith (contrasted with an extremely brutal secular warrior life in both Ireland and England which makes one wonder how anyone survived to sainthood); the inclusion the powerful English abbess Hilda and the Synod of Whitby. Bragg writes about prayer and penitential exercises, and the psychological effects these can have, but steers clear as do most writers on modern Celtic spirituality, of angels, authentic visions, mystical experiences or any of the other expectations of faith in a previous age.

Pagan parallels

Another strand that influenced the Christian expressions of Celtic spirituality can be traced back to the last Celtic Twilight, but it also experienced a sudden expansion of adherents and interested readers in the late twentieth century. This is contemporary Pagan Celtic spirituality. It has many affinities with the Christian movement, and to some extent uses the same sources.

This subject deserves more space and consideration than the brief overview we can give it here. Many practitioners have written on some aspect of the movement, and bookshops often place their works, and sometimes those relating to the more established religions, in the 'Body, Mind and Spirit' sections. In places deeply associated with modern paganism, such as Glastonbury in Somerset or Avebury stone circle in Wiltshire, there are specialist bookshops as well.

Modern paganism is a broad field attracting many different approaches to the spiritual. The numbers of people involved for Ireland are not thought to be high, though some events, for example at the ancient site at Tara, have a media profile. The numbers can only be guessed at for Britain, mainly through the evidence from rituals performed in public, for example at the solstices, or through membership of the Pagan Federation, though many Pagans do not belong it, and not all members have an interest in the 'Celtic' forms. There also appears to be a larger number of people who are attracted to aspects of 'Celtic' paganism but would not necessarily consider themselves to be Pagans or to practice any of the rituals themselves.

Key features of modern paganism in both Britain and Ireland include a reverence for the natural world, and a sense of the divine present in it, which leads to an emphasis on the environmental and ecological aspects of the spiritual. Much modern paganism also contains an understanding of the divine as both male and female, with a strong emphasis in most strands upon the female. There is a sense in most strands that some ancient places have a deeply spiritual significance. Most books on the subject express a belief in personal freedom to act as the individual wishes providing it is not infringing upon the freedom of others. 'And it harm none, do as you will" is often quoted as the central, and indeed the only, doctrine. While the result is a highly individualistic approach to spirituality, many Pagans gather in relatively small groups of like-minded people, and engage jointly in rituals in addition to their private spiritual activities. The occult is nearly always understood in terms of beneficial natural forces, and human energy as something which can be aligned with and can draw upon these energies.

Many Pagans see themselves as recovering an ancient form of religion suppressed by Christianity, and in some cases as modern members of a continuing tradition that went underground for many centuries. This continuity is seen as a generic one rather than something which ran in families. The witch-burning of the seventeenth century is commonly seen as a direct attack upon Pagan practice rather than as a historical phenomenon with social causes. Most Pagans will distinguish themselves firmly from those who practise Satanism or other forms of spirituality that are not nature-based and beneficial in intent.

Solstice, equinox and the Celtic quarter-days provide an eight-fold pattern to the year accepted widely among Pagans and usually marked by local rituals, for example at standing stones or other ancient sites, while there are also some large-scale gatherings, for example at Stonehenge in Wiltshire. Also accepted as valid paths to spiritual development are the use of the signs of Zodiac (sometimes regarded as better-related to the Julian than the Gregorian calendar) and various practices emanating from eastern religions. The emphasis upon personal development has been described as a more severe and developed route than that of organised religion, especially Christianity. There is no general commitment to social action of the kind common among churchgoers.

Although there is considerable interest in the Celtic, the various strands of modern paganism are inclined to be regarded as of equal value and most followers appear to develop their own portfolio of belief and practice. Working upon oneself, sending love out into the world, harming no one else, all seem to be generally accepted and regarded as honourable ways of developing one's own spiritual path. A belief in reincarnation appears to be common. Belief on whether the Goddess or other beings have an independent existence, or whether they are symbolic expressions of the human psyche, varies among Pagans.

As many of the themes of modern Pagan Celtic spirituality have an affinity with those within modern Celtic Christianity, there has inevitably been some overlap and use of the same sources, though not in most cases the use of the same places for rituals. On the whole Christians, particularly those from the more evangelical traditions, have looked warily at these parallel developments, and some would be hostile or nervous at the assumption that they are undertaking similar practices or even sharing beliefs. These concerns are especially acute when this touches on the nature of the divine. Pagan beliefs often tend towards pantheism or to contact with spiritual beings that Christians might consider potentially evil. However, some of the female Christian practitioners sit comfortably with the use of feminine expressions for God that paganism encourages, and many Christians would see the Celtic movement as having helped people to regain the sense of God immanent as well as transcendent. Sometimes the search to balance traditional theological thinking on the natural world and God as Creator, immanent as well as transcendent, is referred to as panentheism, a belief in God present in but not confined to the natural world.

Modern paganism is practised in these forms overwhelmingly by members of the middle classes, and the strong emphasis on liberal self-determination is often associated with regular employment and a generally law-abiding and socially conformist lifestyle. Certain of the tensions perceived within the movement, especially at major celebrations, are between those who see themselves as responsibly practising Pagans, and usually responsible if not necessarily active members of civic society; and those known as New Age Travellers, whose lifestyle is very different but who also engage with solstice events at major ancient sites, often in an enthusiastic and noisy manner. While there is some concern within paganism regarding the danger of damaging those sites, some committed Pagans regard the amount of energy generated at such times as beneficial, and a cause of blessing on the earth.

Study of the Christian as opposed to the Pagan variant of Celtic spirituality has one major advantage in that many of its sources are written. The literary traditions of early Ireland and early Wales were produced by Christian cultures and they have survived because people wrote them down and passed them on. Vestiges of paganism undoubtedly survive in the literary traditions but only as they are seen through Christian eyes. Much more of what can be termed secular survives, and sometimes this have been reinterpreted in Pagan forms, and then presented as the original Pagan tradition which had been submerged by Christianity. An Irish approach can be found in the collections of writings edited by Pádraigín Clancy, *Celtic Threads* (1999), and Patricia Monaghan, *Irish Spirit: Pagan, Celtic, Christian, global* (2001). These take as given that modern Celtic paganism reflects the oldest religion of the island.

Christina Harrington, writing on women in the early Irish church, included in her introduction a section explaining modern beliefs in Celtic spirituality, both Christian and Pagan. She points out that both Christian and Pagan writers on the Celtic are using, in good faith, works from the Victorian era, written when the academic discipline was still young, books which contain concepts that we would no longer include, such as a discussion of whether certain practices or beliefs were 'Pagan survivals'. She points out that Charles Plummer also took this approach in his monumental and still-used collections of the Irish-language and Latin *Lives of the Saints*. Many of the concepts which were drawn on then and are still used today were influenced by the writing of James Frazer, whose two-volume *The Golden Bough* appeared in 1890 and the full 12-volume edition in 1906-15. Frazer compared Christianity to certain world myths, an approach which was both controversial and influential. The divergence of the academic and the popular since the 1930s has meant that these views have stuck. Another source of influence, she points out, has been the feminist movement of the late twentieth century, which seeks a kinder, gentler, more feminine spirituality, an approach which the late nineteenth-century writers did not intend but which can be deduced from their works (Harrington 2002, 5, 7-16)

Conclusions

This chapter has considered some of the dynamics which led to the growth of Celtic spirituality in the late twentieth century, and some of the issues it sought to address in church life, especially the desire to attract people in England to Christianity. We have also considered something of the cultural and political movements of the time, of which the environmental was the most significant; and how in Ireland a rather different set of cultural criteria led to a different form of Celtic Christianity with a stronger affinity to traditional folk literature. The movement also allowed people who felt on the edge of church life while having a committed faith, including women and those attracted to non-traditional forms of church-going, to revitalise their own expressions of faith. There was also, in ways that are not entirely clear, some influence in both directions from modern Celtic-orientated paganism.

CHAPTER FOUR

Themes and perceptions

We now return to some of the themes that have developed as part of Celtic Christianity, to understand more of their attraction and their relevance for the people who developed the movement.

The Trinity
This doctrine is strongly emphasised, and the medieval poems are used to present it in what is seen as a new and palatable manner. Parts of poems like 'Saint Patrick's Breastplate' and similar poems from Welsh medieval tradition are used. Some hymns that were translated and set to music in the late nineteenth century remain popular, such as 'Be thou my vision', usually sung to the Irish tune 'Slane', and Cecil Alexander's rendering of Saint Patrick's Breastplate, 'I bind unto myself today'.

Another source for the emphasis on the Trinity has been the threefold prayers found in Old Irish but more widely known from the Hebridean folk prayers. There are plentiful references to the Trinity, often translated by Carmichael as the 'Triune God', an unusual but comprehensible expression. The Trinity figures in many of the recent prayers written 'in the Celtic tradition' by writers like David Adam, and these have been taken up widely, and his practice copied by other writers.

As the Trinity is central to Christianity, its use is understandable and the attraction for modern writers has been the freshness of expression they have found in the Celtic approach. A sense of the presence of God in every aspect of life is, we have seen, a key feature to what Celtic Christianity is said to offer today, and this is expressed through the Trinity, or through threefold repetition.

The rhythms of life
There are prayers in the *Carmina Gadelica* and similar collections about every daily activity from kindling the morning fire to

waking with nightmares. There are prayers to welcome the new moon and prayers for milking, fishing and travelling. The seasons of the year are marked out, and so the rhythms of human life, from birth and a blessing by the midwife, to chants for reciting to the dying.

Prayers from the *Carmina Gadelica*, and medieval Welsh and Irish poems have been published side by side, to demonstrate the view that the same type of prayer continued across the centuries. They have often been the pattern for new poems composed to reflect modern lifestyles with their very different work patterns.

Esther de Waal, in the two books that gave these prayers to a wider readership and influenced how we respond to them (1988, 1996), sees in them a tradition of praying through the events of daily life which remains significant for us today. New prayers to mark out modern rhythms were composed by David Adam (1989), and many other writers have since written similar prayers that use the cadences and the grammatical forms of the *Carmina Gadelica* to give a powerful sense of difference and yet familiarity. A later book of Adam's takes the approach even further and contains similar prayers specifically designed for use by those in industrial work, particularly in the heavy industries that have since disappeared in Northumbria (1992). Many of the prayers in these and other works by Adam are brief and can be memorised for use during other activities such as driving to work.

Seasonal prayers are similarly popular and whole books are dedicated to them by writers like Shirley Toulson (1996), while the stages of life are also covered in modern prayers by Philip Newell, a former Warden of Iona Abbey and prolific writer and speaker on popular Celtic spirituality (1998).

The use of Hebridean prayers and of these recent works 'in the Celtic tradition', have become part of the common understanding that Celtic spirituality engages with the practicalities of daily life in all its details, that God is to be encountered in all activities, in the world about us, in the passage of the seasons and the stages of our life, and most especially in the dynamics of human relationships. Norman Shanks, a former leader of the Iona Community, speaks for many commentators who have found this sense of presence of God in everyday events:

… Celtic spirituality was not about escape but engagement –
with the humdrum particularities and practicalities of life
(like digging the garden, milking the cow), with the reality of
nature … This was based on a perpetual sense of the presence
of God, on the view that God is to be encountered not only in
the beauty and peace of nature in isolated places, but also in
the immediate, in the rough-and-tumble, in the very middle
of life. (1999, 13)

The power and beauty of the folk prayers and the surviving
older seasonal prayers have a deep effect on modern sensibilities, but they are not essentially different from prayers from
other European popular cultures, especially pre-Reformation
ones. In the early medieval Celtic world they were common too,
and Jackson in his 1935 *Studies in Early Celtic Nature Poetry* de-
voted a chapter to the seasonal poems, including weather prog-
nostications. But it is the prayers from the Hebrides with their
musicality that are best known today. Carmichael saw their
value and recorded them when emigration and the loss of the
language seemed to threaten their survival, and at a time when
much was lost of popular practice and traditions elsewhere.
Less-known to the English writers on Celtic spirituality, similar
prayers were preserved by Douglas Hyde and others in the
Irish-speaking areas of Ireland.

While we do not have a similar collection of prayers in
English, we know a fair amount about England's popular annual
customs, and some of the prayers related to them. These have
not been used in books about Celtic spirituality, perhaps because they were not known to the main writers, or were culturally too medieval and Catholic. It was the freshness and novelty,
the sense of rediscovery, that attracted people to the Hebridean
tradition.

Many other spiritualities engage with the presence of God in
the ordinary rhythms of life, but experience suggests that an emphasis on the turn of the seasons, the events marking it, people's
personal anniversaries and modern national practices, have
proved attractive and useful to people looking for a spiritual
recognition of these and finding them in the Celtic. While they
have been taken from contexts different to the ones in which

they were composed, this approach to the Celtic works. It resonates with a need for pattern in life. It has been common on
events such as retreats for people to write prayers for particular
daily activities, indicating a desire for rhythm in their lives. For
some, there is a spirituality of relationship at work, relationship
with other people, with the natural world and with the divine,
especially the divine perceived as immanent in nature. Further,
some of the poems appear to speak to today's society where the
food we buy is no longer related to seasons, and where as a consequence of climate change the seasons themselves are no
longer predictable.

Nature
As we have seen, the *Carmina Gadelica* was the inspiration for
prayers about the rhythm of life. However, it was medieval
poetry that provided the main sources for the belief promoted
by Allchin, de Waal, the Irish theologian James Mackey, the
Irish poet John O'Donohue and others, that the Celtic ancestors
had an unusually intimate relationship with the natural world.
They made particular use of a small number of early Irish
poems, apparently written by monks, which contain descriptions of the delights of nature and the joys they bring to the
writer. There are similar medieval Welsh poems that delight in
the natural world and express it in ways that we find beautiful
and comprehensible when so much of Celtic literature can be
hard to digest.

Many of the writers we have mentioned have included nature
poetry to support their arguments, and usually supplement the
early written sources with what they see as a continuation of the
same traditions, the prayers and blessings (but not the charms)
from the *Carmina Gadelica*. Most modern writings on Celtic spirituality take it as given that it was through their awareness of the
natural world that the writers of earlier times experienced the
immanence of God, and that they delighted in this.

These poems are certainly very different to the works of the
class of professional poets, composed for a public audience, we
are told while lying in a darkened room, a practice going back to
ancient pre-literate and therefore pre-Christian times. The nature
poems appear to be spontaneous and personal, and conversely

have lasted far longer than the formal professional repertoire intended to extol kings and heroes after their death. They do not give the impression of having been composed in darkened rooms. There was a direct model for them in the many poems praising nature in the Psalter, which the monks recited daily.

There is a great deal written in the Celtic languages which describes the natural world in vivid detail. Most of what is currently used is only a relatively narrow selection from this rich corpus, the early Irish descriptions of the natural world that have a specific religious context and are composed in the first person 'I'. The group, known as 'hermit poetry', consists of several brief marginal notes in manuscripts on other subjects which are notable for their vividness; and a few longer and more consciously literary pieces which incline to the practical. The shorter poems, whether hermit or otherwise, are published together in Greene and O'Connor's anthology (1967, 205-7). The longer 'hermit poems' thank God for nourishment and clothing, and in doing so they mention specifically plants that are edible by humans, or else by the cattle which were the mainstay of the economy and the producers of milk, butter and meat. The authors also rejoice in fresh water, streams abounding in fish, and the sources of clothing, building materials and bedding.

These poems have found a new and enthusiastic audience, and are enjoyed for their beauty, their quirky charm and the apparent spontaneity of the writing. When the practical approach to nature is pointed out to readers, this makes the pleasure richer. The quality of the poems alone gives them an intrinsic value, but again as with the seasonal prayers, love of nature and thanksgiving for food are universal themes and not confined to the Celtic world.

There is also the considerable wealth of Welsh nature poetry, while in Ireland there is a much larger corpus of nature poetry, produced between the eighth and seventeenth centuries and associated with figures such as *Suibhne geilt*, a king who was cursed by a saint and went mad in battle, living wild ever after; and with the pagan warriors of the Fianna, known through the *Duanaire Finn* cycle. While the highly personal-seeming 'hermit poetry' seems to belong to a certain time and to have ceased when a class of professional poet returned in twelfth century

society, the use of nature in the heroic poems continued, sometimes imaginatively placed in the mouth of the speaker, such as
Suibhne, and sometimes directly addressing Christ. While not
prayers in the normal sense, they are part of the corpus. The practical edge remains in this poetry, composed by people dependent
on changes in the natural world, while most of contemporary western society is used to being protected from it. Nature, though always described with great sensitivity, is not always beneficial, for
there are severe frosts, wolves howl, birds freeze and journeys are
dangerous. Though they have been in print for many years, the
poems which emphasise these aspects of nature, even though they
frequently include direct calls upon God for protection, have not
so far been used by writers on Celtic spirituality.

The nature poems have their academic admirers and critics.
Jackson delighted in them and brought them to wider attention,
describing them as 'the best in early Celtic nature poetry, [they]
are concerned most vitally with the singer's own reactions to his
surroundings; not with making a descriptive catalogue about
the various things he sees, but with telling us how he feels about
them, and how they harmonise or clash with his own particular
mood.' (1935, 80.) He also first challenged the belief they were
written by hermits (1935, 179-181). Donnchadh Ó Corráin wrote
as the Celtic movement was getting underway in 1989 a useful
article describing the approach of earlier academics to the poetry.
He suggested that there are only fourteen poems in the 'hermit
poetry' category, and in fact none shows evidence of being composed by a hermit. He proposed that the longer pieces, rather
than being spontaneous expressions of prayer, were composed
nostalgically by residents of the great Irish monastic 'towns' like
Clonmacnois, for a cultured audience. This view was taken up
and developed by Gilbert Markús and Thomas Clancy in their
edition *Iona: the Earliest Poetry of a Celtic Monastery* (1995, 90).
This was intended for the general as well as the academic reader
as a response to modern Celtic spirituality, and their use of Ó
Corráin's views has since appeared in other commentaries critical of the movement. However, Ó Corráin may have overstated
his case, and Markús and Clancy overstated their criticism.
Even in the greatest settlements, the inhabitants were only yards
away from the woods beyond the enclosure.

Whether the practice of prayer through the use of nature continued down the centuries to emerge to our view again in the late nineteenth-century folk poems, is impossible to tell. However, a direct connection between the poems of the different periods is claimed, and recent books often present them side by side. While the intimacy and freshness of expression in both the earlier and later poetry seem unique to the Gaelic-speaking world, the earlier writers had the advantage of the scriptures, especially the Book of Psalms as part of the rhythm of their own daily lives. So did many others across Europe and it seems unlikely that the contents are greatly different from prayers composed in non-Celtic cultures.

There is another aspect to these poems which has not been explored, their praise for the orderliness of the monastic life. Celtic monasticism was rigorous, with long hours spent praying, communally and in private, the daily recitation of the psalms, mostly from memory, limited food, sleep and social contact, and a strong penitential tradition. A few contemporary writers refer to these aspects of life and to the direct dependence on a successful annual harvest, and freedom from plague, famine and tempest. Most concentrate on a belief that the hermits had spontaneous access to the divine, that they desired to live simply and closely to nature to refine this, and that, even when living with others, they were free of burdensome ecclesiastical structures. Most of these matters reflect contemporary concerns over the environment and how people can live more lightly, and alsoan ideal of a more rural lifestyle, issues that find a model in the little that is known about the way of life of early Christian hermits. They were rediscovered mainly by clergymen in increasingly bureaucratic churches.

The emphasis on the natural world is one of the best-known aspects of Celtic spirituality. While modern writers may have been originally attracted by the quality of the poetry and its perceived quaintness, our increasing concerns about climate change mean that this aspect of the movement is likely to develop further, and prayers in religious services written 'in the Celtic tradition' are common. These concerns does not have seen to have led to direct campaigning on environmental or ecological issues, though it might have contributed to more thought about lifestyles and travel.

Either because of their attractiveness, or simply because they have been popularised in the last generation, the ancient poems and the more recent folk poetry from the Hebrides are now well-known in contemporary Christian circles. As we have seen, they are not unique. Helen Waddell presented similarly moving nature poetry composed on the early medieval continent, in *The Wandering Scholars* and in her collection and translation of the poetry, *Medieval Latin Lyrics* (1929), while poets down the centuries have been moved to describing the natural world and the religious sentiments it arouses. A relatively recent Irish example, sometimes quoted, is the poem 'I see his blood upon the rose' by Joseph Plunkett, executed as a leader of the 1916 Easter Rising, and whose works are familiar to many in Ireland from their schooldays.

Many of those who use works such as the Hebridean poetry of the *Carmina Gadelica* see the sense of God present in nature as one of the major gifts of the movement. Matters as basic to human existence as the natural world and the turn of the seasons are likely to continue to inspire poets, whether they take as their muse the Celtic tradition or not, and whether they are from Ireland or Italy. This aspect of the folk tradition is established as something exceptional, and the quality continues to attract new readers.

Saints

We not only have acute first-person descriptions of the natural world, but also accounts of some of the people who lived in this close proximity to the natural world in the early centuries of Christianity in Ireland and Britain.

The fascination with the saints is perhaps one of the more surprising aspects of a movement initiated largely by evangelicals. They have been the subject of several books that retell anecdotes about them or the places they came from, by writers such as the priest Michael Rodgers and Marcus Losack in their *Glendalough: a Celtic Pilgrimage* (1996) and Helen Julian in *Lindisfarne Icon: St Cuthbert and the 21st century Christian* (2004). More specific works include Ian Bradley's 1996 book on Saint Columba of Iona, published just before the fifteen-hundredth anniversary of his death.

Most of these books are not written from a Catholic perspective and do not usually contain prayers to, or even the assumption that we should pray to, the saints. Instead, saints are presented as models with whom we can emphasise. This allows enjoyment of the stories about them as parables without opening up possibly divisive interpretations of how we should address them. The life-stories of the saints also provide the opportunities, used by David Adam and the Northumbria Community writers among others, to weave retreats and meditations around them.

One of the main sources for the saints is not in the normal sense Celtic at all, but is the Englishman Bede's Latin *Ecclesiastical History of the English People*. Another source is Adamnán's *Life of Saint Columba*, while numerous commentators use the accounts of other early English, Irish and Welsh historians and hagiographers to relate, or reflect upon, the stories of lesser-known saints. These stories are frequently whimsical and quite possibly originally meant in part as warning against not taking certain religious practices too far, as in the case of Cuthbert, who spent nights in the North Sea, or Kevin who spent so long praying with his arms outstretched that a blackbird laid her eggs in his hand. Modern writers usually present these stories as *exempla*, parables, to be understood spiritually rather than as fact or warning, and certainly not as mockery.

Saint Patrick emerges strongly in the movement, mainly as a missionary and as one who had suffered. He is also sometimes used as a model of the spiritual warrior, who defeated the forces of evil at Easter. Interestingly for a movement where being on the edge is so important, he speaks of his life in Ireland as on the edge, outside the Roman Empire. According to Thomas O'Loughlin, his missionary activity in bringing Ireland into the community of believers and the known world, was hastening the Second Coming, for once the gospel had been preached to the ends of the earth, there was nothing to hold it back (O'Loughlin 2005, 72-8). Other significant saints include Ninian of Whithorn, who provides a native Scottish model of mission and pastoral care.

Saint Bridget is understandably popular as a female model, the leader of a double monastery of male and female religious, adviser to clerics and ruler of a household. As one of the roles of the saints is to welcome the stranger, to provide hospitality as well as advice, she is seen as a patron of hospitality, one who increases the supply of butter in particular. Her domestic associations have proved popular, as has the tradition that, though born centuries later, she was a midwife to Jesus. Irish writers often emphasise her continuing association with food, the hearth, and provision for strangers, and it remains the practice in parts of Donegal to first-foot and to leave food out on the eve of her festival, 1 February. A returning practice across Ireland is making rush crosses in her honour.

Very popular are the stories of Saint Columba's leaving Ireland and founding a monastery from which Christianity was brought to parts of Scotland and northern England. As both Iona and Northumbria's Holy Island are today again places of pilgrimage, he is an ideal model. The early poems commemorating him treat him as an exile and penitent, who delighted in the beauty of his adoptive home but also yearned for Ireland. The stories describe him welcoming pilgrims, both human and on one occasion avian, when a crane arrived from Ireland needing his attention. Iona in his time is presented as the hub of missionary activity, including the mission to the Picts on which he encountered an ancestor of the Loch Ness monster. Columba's role as a spiritual guide whom people travelled to consult, gives him an exceptional status as a soul-friend, an *anam-chara*.

Donald Meek addressed, in an academic article (1999) and in a more popular book (2000), the many different ways in which Columba and other saints have been reinterpreted to suit the demands of different historical periods, and the problems associated with making 'Celtic' saints role-models to suit contemporary church needs. However, in the case of the saints, most modern writers make an attempt to use ancient sources in a manner that reflects the context in which they lived. The poetic prayers attributed to Columba are genuinely ancient, as are Adamnán's descriptions of monastic life, and these are used by modern writers, even if they are not familiar with the historical and literary or theological contexts of the original poems.

Many writers, like de Waal, seek to understand and recover popular local traditions about the saints, even if these have survived only in a weakened form. This may bring them to the question of whether to directly address the saints. The *Carmina Gadelica* contains many invocations, prayers in particular to Saints Columba and Bridget and the Archangels, and also litanies containing the names of numerous saints and angels. De Waal selected only a handful for her anthology *The Celtic Vision* (1988), mainly from those addressed to Saints Bridget and Michael. Several of these are requests for aid associated with their traditional specialised roles rather than prayers that directly ask them to intercede with God. This means there is a fine line between them and some of the 'charms' also contained in the *Carmina Gadelica* which de Waal does not include in a book aimed specifically at the religious market. She also avoided those prayers where the repetitive wording is close to the 'charms'.

Most of Carmichael's prayers to the saints were collected from the Catholic population on South Uist and in his time prayers invoking saints belonged, at least officially, only to the Catholic areas of the Gaelic-speaking world. While de Waal provides references to her sources, she and similar writers who treat these prayers as part of a common tradition, may be unintentionally harvesting what they want, regardless of the culture of a poem's home territory.

De Waal gives prominence to one particular saint who is otherwise largely neglected by writers on Celtic spirituality. Although the saints are used primarily as models, significantly absent from most books are references to the Virgin Mary. This may be through fear that the boundaries between emulation, using someone's life as a model, and intercession, praying to them to intercede with God, might become too thin. However, devotion to Mary is a major part of Irish spirituality of any period, from the eighth century lament of the poet Blathmac to insular versions of the European lament of Mary at the foot of the cross, to the *Carmina Gadelica*, to modern Irish blessings.

In fact Blathmac's poem gives us a direct evidence of the spirituality of the early monks. Addressing Mary directly, Blathmac focuses on the crucifixion and laments with her for Jesus. His poem, which takes fifteen minutes to recite, is, he tells us in stanza 140, to be used morning and evening as a breastplate and protection. He recommends it be said while fasting on Friday evening (stanza 141). This fine poem and instructions on how to recite it are one of the few direct examples of early Christian spiritual practice. It has not been taken up by contemporary writers, either because they are not aware of it or because it does not fit with contemporary sensibilities.

The near-absence of references to Mary is significant for another reason. Contemporary Celtic tradition presents the sexes as equal in the early 'Celtic Church', and this is one of the ways that make it attractive for Christians today. Every other woman from these islands or beyond, who can reasonably be regarded as saintly, is treated as a role model, and each is given as much attention as possible in an effort to secure a gender balance that neither the scriptures nor the corpus of saints' lives provide. English books give special prominence to Hilda of Whitby, while most books give space to Saint Brigit and Saint Ita, a more localised midwife and nurse to Jesus. Little-known Irish saints including the formidable Cannera (Conaire) and Samthann, who led a monastic community, are also given attention to redress the gender balance (Marsh and Bamford 1986, 76-8, Adam 2000). Both appear in the Northumbria Community's *Celtic Daily Prayer*.

Christina Harrington (2002, 15) has noted that modern paganism pays little attention to prominent women saints, with the exception of Saint Brigit, who is regarded as a christianisation of a pre-Christian Goddess. In the case of women saints, it seems that Christian Celtic spirituality is broader than its pagan counterpart. It takes its models, though, only from Christian saints and does not use other prominent female figures of early Irish literature. For example, the much anthologised Old Woman of Beare, who is better known than many of these female saints, is not included in modern books on spirituality, for her pagan ancestry and penitential approach does not fit with being a role model. She is omitted at one end of the spectrum, while Mary the mother of Jesus, is practically absent at the other.

Finally, it is significant that the modern movement does not refer to living people as saints, as sometimes happened in early Christian times. But the Northumbria Community's *Celtic Daily Prayer* and certain other collections include living people who might be considered models for us today, though neither they, nor others who have recently died, are actually called saints. There are also no examples of saints acting vindictively, a feature of early Irish and Welsh sainthood that sits uneasily with our expectations today.

The soul-friend

Many of the stories about the saints depicted them as spiritual guides. This is especially true of Saint Columba, who is described in this role in the biography written by his successor, the third abbot of Iona, Adamnán. Others also act in ways compatible with being a spiritual guide, including Saint Hilda of Whitby.

While the current Celtic movement expresses great yearning for reintegration, harmony with the natural world and community with fellow believers, it is also associated with the desire for solitude and individual prayer. Many of the *Lives of the Saints* concern hermits or, more usefully for people today, saints who live part of their lives as hermits. One theme taken up frequently by writers is the belief that all serious spiritual seekers in early Celtic times, had an *anam-chara*, an expression meaning a soul-friend which is spelt in a number of ways that reflect Old, Modern and reconstructed Irish. The *anam-chara* was often mentioned in early texts, but the concept was more that of a confessor, and it is generally believed by scholars of the period that this Irish practice led to the pattern of the private confession of sins that became a standard part of western Christianity.

It may therefore help to consider the original context. The soul-friend was there as an adviser but also to provide medicine for the soul, in terms of penances, some of which were by current standards very severe, but which were intended to restore the soul to health in the same way as often rigorous medical prescription was intended to restore the body to health. Sometimes a group of people might live together in an isolated place, exiled from normal society and the reception of the sacraments until they were ready to have completed their spiritual treatment and return as healthy members of Christian society. From these practices came a series of *penitentials*, guides for confessors, that prescribed the amount of penance suited to all conceivable, and some inconceivable, sins, depending on their gravity and on who had committed the sin.

This aspect of early Irish and indeed Welsh and English society is one of these least digestible to people today and is often

omitted in books on Celtic spirituality, though some writers, including Ian Bradley and Thomas O'Loughlin, have tried to find
some contemporary use for it. While the legalistic aspects of
these texts may be unattractive, and the idea of adjudicating for
each sin rather than seeking a general forgiveness may be ab-
horrent, the penitentials are based upon legal considerations in
the societies that formed them. In fact, in their time they may
have been a radical break with accepted practice. In the highly
stratified societies in which they appeared, much legal adjudica-
tion for crimes depended on the status of the individual offended
and the price of their honour. Therefore, the legal penalties were
higher when a person of low status offended a king, for example
by insulting them or killing one of their relatives. However,
should a king undertake similar action against someone of low
status, he would be required to pay less in recompense. The penitentials at times take the opposing view. The penalties for sin,
crime against the highest authority, God, the high-king of heav-
en, are much less for a child than for an abbot where sexual sin is
concerned. At times, the greater the status and responsibility, the
greater the need for spiritual medicine, and the greater the capacity should be to take it. The penance for some sins is higher for a
cleric than for a lay person.

Legal texts in these societies were statements of an ideal. The
responsibility for enforcing the law was usually dependant
upon the most powerful person, usually the king. In the penitentials, enforcement on the whole was dependant on the sin-
ning individuals, with the help of their confessor and friends,
especially the penitent's friends and superiors in a monastic
community. But the penitentials also imply that everyone, including slaves and small children, had a spiritual identity, even
where their legal identity was non-existent, or nearly so. It was
in this context that we might need to consider the development
of the *anam-chara*.

It is clear from the stories about the saints like Columba that
they were used as advisers, for consultation and discernment on
other matters than sin. It is clear too that certain lay people, men
and women, had *anam-chairde*. It has been suggested that the role
of *anam-chara* owes something to that of the personal adviser to a
king, but was made available to a wider range of people.

Interestingly, at least one prominent early Christian woman, the Irish abbess Samthann, seems to have been used, including by male saints, as such an adviser. However, one story of her own quest for an *anam-chara* indicates an awareness of the potentially fraught nature of such relationships between members of the opposite sexes.

The term *anam-chara* is usually used today to mean something more approximate to this advisory role, someone with whom the individual has the opportunity for private and confidential discussion on one's life, spiritual and otherwise. This modern adviser is unlikely to take the directive attitude found in the *Lives of the Saints*, nor to impose penances. This lies well with individual spiritual direction as developed recently from the Ignatian spiritual tradition, and is in some ways similar to mentoring in the more evangelical traditions.

The ideal of having a soul-friend is presumably in part to balance the frequently-expressed desires for both individualism and the community, and these must also have been an issue in early monastic experience, if expressed in different terms. Whether the current approach to the soul-friend has much to do with early Christian practice may be questioned, but the association the word provides is encouraged by key proponents like Ray Simpson (1999, 2003, 17-25), and it seems a valued experience for many people engaged in the movement or in other modern expressions of Christian spirituality.

Place and Protection

While one traditional role of the saint was to provide spiritual counsel, another was to provide hospitality and refuge at a holy place, and another was to provide protection.

Monastic sites were traditionally places of refuge from those pursued by enemies, places for exiles to stay, places of hospitality for travellers, and places of surplus food during times of hardship. The stories of the saints also suggest that they were places where knowledge could be sought, and they are frequently referred to as places where wealthy people chose to end their lives in penitence. Both rich and poor sought to be buried in such places, the protection of the saint applying after death as much as during life. The provision of hospitality for those in need is also seen to have beneficial consequences, for it sometimes led to personal contacts and reciprocal social dues. Iona provided a place of refuge for the exiled Northumbrian prince Oswald of Northumbria in the early seventh century. On gaining his kingdom he invited monks of Iona to preach Christianity there.

There are numerous protective prayers, including the groups known as *loricae*, 'breastplates', which are said to have derived in part from older protective charms. They spread to other languages, including Old English, where they are sometimes classified as charms. Whatever their possible pre-Christian origins, the term 'breastplate' and the similar martial imagery indicates that the writers in the warrior societies that produced them were inspired by the scriptures, in particular Paul's First Letter to the Thessalonians 5:8:

> But since we belong to the day, let us be self-controlled, putting on faith and love as a breastplate, and the hope of salvation as a helmet;

and the better-known text in his Letter to the Ephesians 6:14-17:

> Stand firm then, with the belt of truth buckled around your waist, with the breastplate of righteousness in place, and with your feet fitted with the readiness that comes from the gospel of peace. In addition to all this, take up the shield of faith, with which you can extinguish all the flaming arrows of the evil one. Take the helmet of salvation and the sword of the Spirit, which is the word of God. (*New International Version*)

The most beautifully constructed and best-known, the eighth-century 'Saint Patrick's Breastplate' or 'Cry of the Deer', also appears to owe much to the ancient Christian hymn, the *Te Deum*. It is also cited as an example of the emphasis on the Trinity in modern Celtic spirituality and an example of the closeness of the Celts to nature. This prayer and others like it must have been important when travel was dangerous due to weather, wolves and hostile tribes.

There are many other simpler prayers for protection, both in the medieval written traditions, and in the folk tradition as known through the *Carmina Gadelica*. One specific form of prayer derived from Carmichael has been regarded as giving direct personal protection by providing a sacred space around an individual, even while they are travelling. Like many such prayers, it is deemed to have been current in early Christian times too.

In a section on protection poetry, Carmichael gives three of what he calls *Caim* prayers, which call upon the Trinity or saints (*Carmina Gadelica* iii, 102-7). He describes the *Caim* as made by a person turning sun-wise with the right forefinger outstretched, and drawing an imaginary circle, while asking for protection within the circle (iii, 102-3.) As the person moves forward, the circle and its protection move too, safeguarding the person within it. Carmichael specifically distinguishes the *Caim* prayer from a charm and assures the reader that both Catholics and Protestants use it.

He translated the word both as 'compassing' and 'guarding', but this form of prayer is not known outside of Carmichael's work. The word *Caim* is recorded in one Gaelic dictionary, that of Edward Dwelly in 1901-11, but Dwelly may have taken it from Carmichael, and it does not appear in Irish dictionaries. Seán Ó Duinn, writing in Irish, refers to *Caim* prayers in a section on popular 'breastplates', but the three examples he gives are Carmichael's (Ó Duinn 1990, 151-2). Therefore, we cannot know if this was a popular practice, or was something done only by a small number of people, who had perhaps learnt it from each other. There is a European folk tradition of producing a protective circle about a person, often to ward off the devil, so this may have been a variant rather than anything essentially Celtic. Carmichael elsewhere glosses the word, giving examples of its use to mean a 'sanctuary', or an 'encompassing' by Christ or a saint, and states that the making of a *caim* is 'not confined to illiterates or Catholics. A distinguished scholar and a rigid Protestant told me that he often found himself unconsciously making the "caim".' Carmichael goes on to relate a story where a young girl is saved from a water-horse and destruction because a priest makes a *caim* around her. (*Carmina Gadelica* ii, 240-1.)

But the tradition, if it was one, seems to speak to current concerns, for it has been taken up extensively by contemporary writers, such as David Adam, who calls these prayers, using

Carmichael's notes, 'encompassing' prayers. Ian Bradley regarded them as pre-Christian in origin, but also related to the *loricae*, breastplate prayers and suitable for contemporary Christians (1993, 47). The Community of Aidan and Hilda based on Holy Island, which gives retreats and publishes books on Celtic spirituality, has a governing body called the Caim Council.

The need for the protection of the Trinity and the saints, and the belief that the protection moves with the person, are clearly felt relevant for today. Contemporary western lifestyles involve much travelling, and while this is probably physically safer than many daily Hebridean activities, such as egg-collecting on sea-cliffs, it involves moving among strangers. Recently-composed *Caim* prayers are frequently used together with the journey blessings which can generally be taken directly from the *Carmina Gadelica*.

The protection prayers may also supply a need in a rootless society where tracing one's ancestors, or knowing who previously lived in the family home are increasingly popular, and they possibly parallel secular activities.

Protection prayers are sometimes referred to in modern books written from an evangelical perspective, as being useful in situations of 'spiritual warfare' where protection from evil forces is needed. The folk prayers and their modern variants are taken with excerpts from the lives of saints and seen as part of an ancient tradition of warring against these evil forces to claim places as well as people for Christ. Ancient prayers such as Saint Patrick's Breastplate are seen as both evidence of this warfare and protection against it. The story is often recounted of Saint Patrick converting Ireland to Christianity. On the way to visit the high-king, an ambush had been set for him but as his party passed by all his enemies saw were deer. Patrick sang the Breastplate in thanksgiving, and continued his journey, defeating the forces of paganism at Tara that Easter. Holy places, as written about by among others Ray Simpson of the Community of Aidan and Hilda (2003, 9-16) who writes from a High-Church Anglican perspective, can be seen as having a role in providing respite from spiritual warfare.

More, in addition to the intrinsic sense of place they provide, some religious sites are felt to contain inherent protection, because deep prayer has occurred there over the centuries. Visiting such places and deriving spiritual benefit from the journey as well as the arrival, have a long tradition in Christianity and are a major feature of the contemporary Celtic movement.

Pilgrimage
Several kinds of pilgrimage can be found in early medieval sources, but not all are equally well-used at present. Most used today are the stories of monks who went away as missionaries, founding places that are now the focus of pilgrimage. Saint Columba and the Iona monk Aidan, who founded the Lindisfarne monastery, are the main models. Columba is often described as having undertaken the journey in penance, one of the forms of martyrdom defined by the early Irish church. A later account of his life sees his exile as the consequence of having caused a battle in Ireland. This account and the themes of exile and new foundations, assisted by some of the poetry attributed him, have been used widely as models for mission. However, the continental insular missions, undertaken by the seventh-century Irish saint Columbanus and others, have proved much less popular. De Waal has used Waddell's writings (1927, 1929) on the continental missions and Martin Robinson (2000) considers them when looking at modern forms of mission, but they have not had widespread influence, perhaps because late twentieth-century Continental Europe was not seen, as Britain was, as mission territory. Aspects modern writers have not taken into the movement's canon are the accounts of medieval pilgrimages to Rome and Jerusalem, though it is from Irish royal pilgrimages of the tenth and eleventh centuries that some of the poetry has come.

Other kinds of pilgrimage are mentioned by most modern writers on the Celtic, and several take it as their main theme. Influential writers such as de Waal, and Bradley in his 1993 book *The Celtic Way*, devote whole sections to it. De Waal also drew attention to those who went into exile for the love of God, to remote hermitages and uninhabited islands (1991, 53-4). Isolated monasteries such as the collection of beehive huts on Sceilg Mhichíl, Skellig Michael, a rocky outcrop eight miles west of County Kerry in Ireland, is one such place. The Anglo-Saxon

Saint Cuthbert who, after a life as bishop, took up residence and an austere lifestyle on the Farne Islands is another model, while Saint Cedd who made his base at Bradwell-on-Sea in Essex, created a place that has become the focus of pilgrimage.

The ultimate pilgrim has left few places we can easily visit, though the voyages of the Irish Saint Brendan are frequently used as the basis for devotions and poems. He made journeys west across the sea, meeting hermits on remote islands and en-countering natural wonders, many of them similar to those found in older, secular, wonder literature of Ireland with its happy otherworld west over sea. The turn of the seasons and the marvels he encounters are treated by contemporary comment-ators as parables and a means of reflection on one's own spiritual life. David Adam uses this theme in *A desert in the ocean* (2000), a reflection on a medieval poem he attributes to Saint Brendan, while the Northumbria Community's Daily Office also contains meditations on the theme. Another approach has been suggested by Thomas O'Loughlin, who points to the strong liturgical and penitential tradition of the early medieval voyages of Brendan and others (2000a, 177-8, 2000b, 91-7).

The Brendan legend belongs to a group of early Irish voyage tales. Another, *The Voyage of Bran*, though written in the Christian period, makes the journey one to a pagan otherworld of delight, as do a handful of poems in which a human is invited to the otherworld to the west. These tales were meant for entertain-ment, but there are other prose tales, such as the voyages of Mael Dúin and the Uí Chorra, which are clearly religious in in-tent. Translations of parts of all of these voyages have been available for many years in Jackson's *A Celtic Miscellany*, (1951, 1971), but have not been used by recent writers on the Celtic.

Pilgrimage on Saint Brendan's scale is no longer available to us, and the lands to the west now belong to the geographically identifiable world rather than that of wonder-tale. However, the desire to be a pilgrim remains strong, and there are various op-portunities available which include something of the medieval package of travel with spiritual input and assist people or groups to journey to some special place, to absorb the atmosphere, to pray, to take time away from routine activities, and to return re-freshed. Modern Christian pilgrimage can include these elements together with a degree of comfort. The Celtic movement speaks to the desire to go on pilgrimage, and although these events are usually small-scale, it may be wondered whether modern urban dwellers' exposure to the much larger-scale and rigorous Muslim *haj*, the pilgrimage to Mecca, might have rekindled the desire to make spiritual journeys. While the austerity of the early pilgrims and the saints they visited has not been emulated, some people make a physical effort that may include actions like walking across the sands to Holy Island.

Traditional pilgrimages to holy wells and similar sites still occur in parts of Scotland, Wales and Ireland, and some of these remain physically rigorous. While people may go in groups, perhaps on the annual saint's 'pattern', patronal, day, they may also go privately and the practice of reciting prayers while walking in traditional paths around the well is frequently performed individually. These relatively local affairs have regained popularity in Ireland, while the annual climb of Croagh Patrick in County Mayo on the last Sunday in July, and the Lough Derg penitential pilgrimage, are expanding. 'Climbing the reek' has become controversial due to the number of accidents and exposure to hypothermia that have occurred as inexperienced urban dwellers have come unprepared; and the traditional barefoot climb is discouraged though still done by a few. The barefoot Lough Derg pilgrimage, on an island in the County Donegal lake, is more structured, and remains an overwhelmingly Catholic practice

Ó Duinn recommends 'patterns' in his book for an Irish-speaking audience (1990, 157-61) and another Irish writer, O'Loughlin, makes the connection between them and ancient circular prayer (2000a, 151-9). These traditional practices, even the large-scale and publicised ones, have not been taken into Celtic spirituality, but remain within the realms of the popular vernacular culture. The intercessions to the saints which are part of the communal devotions that take place may be too alien for evangelical English Christians, but it may simply be that they do not know about them.

Places of spiritual pilgrimage known to followers of Celtic spirituality may provide simple but comfortable accommodation, attractive to people on a moderate income. Many of the destinations welcome children, making them suitable for family, or church, holidays. What they provide may be different to pilgrimages to remote islands, to Rome and Jerusalem, or to the local holy well, but they play a major part in today's Celtic movement.

Women and the Celtic
Early accounts of pilgrimages are almost all about male pilgrims. Women saints figure frequently as hosts, providers and spiritual advisors, and the current movement tends strongly to portraying women as equal in status to men in early Celtic society. Although Helen Waddell in her *Wandering Scholars* mentions women being banned from going on pilgrimage – a ban which indicates that they were doing it – contemporary writers like de Waal are more likely to quote, as Ian Bradley does (1993, 80), the comment attributed to Samthann, abbess of Clonbroney: 'Were God to be found overseas, I too would take ship and go. But since God is near to all that call upon him, there is no constraint upon us to seek him overseas. For from every land there is a way to the kingdom of heaven.' The quote has the additional advantages of emphasising her role as adviser, and as a person who holds authority and makes her own choices.

Some writers take into account the ancient pre-Christian goddesses, their possible association with holy wells, and their affinity with natural features of the landscape. In 1989 an Irish writer Mary Condren suggested that an ancient, peaceful, woman-centred religion was edged out by an authoritarian male church. While this view may owe a certain amount to outdated scholarship of the kind Harrington describes (2002, 9), it gained some popularity in Ireland.

The equality of women in early Ireland and Wales is not supported by historical evidence and the saints who appear in either ancient or modern writings are often of royal origins, though some may not have existed at all. However, the position of women today is unlikely to be challenged, for gender equality is a non-negotiable theme, and one of the expected roles of Celtic spirituality is to provide evidence that the position of women was better in earlier times. Most of the men whose writings led to the development of the current Celtic movement

were coming from an evangelical perspective that showed limited interest in women's roles, but the women writers, mainly educated professionals, reflected female expectations in the late
twentieth century. The divide between scholarship and expectations is particularly wide here, and Harrington's assessment of
the actual position of women, in particular nuns, in the early
churches in the Celtic lands is far less known or influential than
Condren's popular feminist reconstruction.

Social and cultural changes in twentieth-century Ireland and
England formed the view expressed by Condren, and many others,
of the role of women in early Christian Ireland. Consciously or
not, ancient texts are selected and interpreted to support the
modern viewpoint. On one hand, beneath the desire to believe
that women were equal in the 'Celtic Church' is criticism of the
current, unequal, position of women in the church, particularly
in the Catholic Church. At another level, there is a view that
Celtic spirituality is, or should be, more feminine in its spiritual
essence than the Christianity received through the traditional,
male-led denominations, more earthed in domestic life and private
practices, more gentle, poetic and encompassing. This belief in
the position of women is largely the result of twentieth-century
enthusiasts reading contemporary concerns into sixth-century
Ireland, and reflects more our current need for role-models than
the historical evidence.

One unusual aspect related to the role of women concerns a
legal tract by the third abbot of Iona, Adamnán, *The Law of the
Innocents*. This text, which was translated recently by Gilbert
Márkus (1997), provides for the protection of children and other
non-combatants in times of strife, and exempts women from
military service. The modern Celtic movement depicts the original Christians of Adamnán's time as peace-loving and extols the
feminine. The expectations and concerns of contemporary
women and our knowledge of his time means that the gap between the historical and the desired is very wide here. However,
in 2001 an anti-nuclear activist, Angie Zelter, intended to use
The Law of the Innocents as part of a legal defence on non-violent
action against the use of nuclear weapons. As the case was dis-
missed before this defence could be presented, it remains
untested, but provides a potential example of a new use for an

old text. However, a degree of selectivity might have applied, for Adamnán's other prescriptions include both men and women being set adrift alone in a boat, to go where the wind blows them, as the penalty for certain grievous crimes. This is also found in other early law texts, and may have resonated with exile and penitential pilgrimage for the original audience, but hardly does so for a modern one; and the extent to which this tract can be used to raise the position of women is at best unclear.

Although there are historical problems with the view of women as equals in the early churches in these islands, the common expectations today are that women should be equal in the churches, and stories are selected to give this sense of equality to the past as well. In fact, their position touches on another issue regarding authority and hierarchy in church life. Women in the 'Celtic' world are most obviously represented by early saints, and one of these is given a key role in a subject that is central to understanding the modern English form of Celtic Christianity.

The Synod of Whitby

Celtic enthusiasts in England take as factual that at the Synod of Whitby in 664, a peace-loving, individualistic and locally-rooted 'Celtic Church' was overwhelmed by a continental, Romanising church which stifled much of its creativity. Contemporary Celtic Christianity is viewed in nearly every book written from an English perspective as seeking to redress the damage and return to a purer, happier form of worship, community and spirituality. This issue has become a theme in itself, an injustice heaped upon the Celtic church, and it is seen as a defining moment and a reason to resist pressures imposed from outside in the interests of a dull conformity.

The main historical source for the Synod of Whitby is Bede's *Ecclesiastical History of the English People*, in which the debate centred on whether the church in Northumbria should adopt the continental dating of Easter, the continental tonsure and a few similar practices. Bede, writing three generations after the event, makes the Synod, held at the royal foundation of Whitby which was governed by Saint Hilda, the high point of his *History*. He presents the issues as coming to a head because in Northumbria the king and queen were following differing practices. Bede believed that in adopting continental practice his nation was brought into line with the universal church, that the move started a process of unifying the Saxon kingdoms, and that it would hopefully in time do the same for the other Christian nations surrounding his own, the Picts, Scots, Irish, and even the Britons of Wales, whom he particularly disliked. The account in his *History* is not in our sense a historical record but his literary creation, perhaps based in part on the memories of those who were present.

Modern writers treat the subject of the Synod as a matter of who held 'authority' in church life, and so the relevance of the debate in its own time, and the reasons why Bede gave so much space to it, are often lost. The historian Caitlin Corning points out in her recent work (2006: 9-14) that the dating was a matter of ensuring the same standards universally, so that all Christians could worship together at the same time, with scriptural readings and periods of feasting and fasting coinciding. These were significant matters at a time of rapid evangelism, and they had theological implications for the nature of the universal church, the Body of Christ, which it was believed should function as a whole. Standardisation was a means too of overcoming practical difficulties like those experienced at the Northumbrian court.

The issues surrounding constructing an Easter table are complex, referring as they do to Jewish practice, to calculations on when the equinox occurs in the Julian calendar, and to the phases of the moon. Theologically, Easter was to occur at a time when day was longer than night, when Christ, the Light of the World, redeemed the world. Over the years, calculations had been undertaken in different places at different times and were inevitably at variance with each other. A secondary debate focused on the tonsure, the clerical haircut, which was a sign of status for clerics, just as other forms of haircut were signs of status for other social groups. The traditional insular form had been to shave the head across the front while the continental practice was to shave a circular patch on the scalp. While this issue was addressed separately in some other places, like Iona, where the continental dating for Easter was adopted three years before the continental tonsure, at Whitby both subjects were debated together, and the tonsure became a visible sign of allegiance to one party or the other.

The Synod was a Northumbrian event. It affected the other Saxon kingdoms because the decisions made there led to the Synod of Hertford in 673, where they were adopted for all the Saxon kingdoms. The decision at Whitby had no direct effect in the Celtic-speaking lands, though they must have added impetus to a developing trend. The dating of Easter was certainly contentious in Ireland but its synods are recorded more cryptically and without the benefit of a dramatic storyteller like Bede. Parts of southern Ireland had adopted continental practice some time beforehand, while those parts further from the continent adopted it later (Corning 2006, 4-14). The letter of Cummian in 632-633 to the abbot Ségéne of Iona encouraging the community to adapt the new dating, speaks of the ancient version brought to Ireland by Saint Patrick (O'Loughlin 2005, 101). Northumbria was an important centre for the spread of Christianity, but the decision did not end communications between Iona and Lindisfarne, and seems to have been more of a psychological blow than something which had practical implications, matters that the historian Máire Hebert has explored in her study of Iona and its affiliated monasteries (1996, 44-6). Iona eventually adopted the continental dating for Easter in 716, while in Wales the traditional dating was retained longer.

The Synod of Whitby has been used in England since the Reformation as an example of a native church with a purer form of Christianity being overcome by Rome. For modern writers, the issues are about authority. This approach presents the 'Roman' party, those in favour of following continental practice, as winning due to the forceful but unjust arguments put forward by their key speaker, Wilfred. The 'Celtic Church', which is usually regarded as very individualistic but in this context is treated as a unified body, then succumbed to Roman authority.

This interpretation has several consequences. One is that a Romanising church is seen as imposing itself on the other churches. This does not sit comfortably with modern expectations regarding ecumenism and freedom of conscience, or even with ecumenical courtesy. Another consequence is that we have to skip over the many intervening centuries, and relate what we think and feel today to what was happening in the very different society of the seventh century. It also takes as read that church life in

England today (except perhaps in the independent churches), is unable to meet people's needs and spiritual aspirations and that this is why it attracts fewer and fewer people. A return to the spontaneous, freer, more joyful early church of these islands would, it follows, attract people to the Christian faith. Another consequence is to increase the role Hilda played. In Bede's account she hosted the Synod, but many contemporary books declare that she convened and chaired it and acted as a peacemaker afterwards. These roles sit well with present-day interpretations of the position of women, but there is no evidence that they were true.

Bede is highly regarded by writers on Celtic spirituality, but is seen as misguided in the case of the Whitby decision, of which he approved. The Synod is presented as a tragedy, a time when uniformity overcame spontaneity. There is no reason to believe that it caused major upheaval at the time, however, and the years following Whitby saw no discernable changes in spiritual or secular culture but the production of the great Gospel Books, including the Lindisfarne Gospels, the shrine and fabrics from Cuthbert's grave, and liturgical vessels of high craftsmanship. They also saw the flowering of English prose and poetry, including Bede's own prodigious output and the work of his contemporaries.

There may be another reason for the emphasis on this Synod in contemporary English Celtic Christianity, a distrust of overarching political and administrative organisations. The largest of these is the European Union, a political and economic entity whose powers are frequently regarded negatively in Britain. Against the might of a similar institution, the Roman church that grew out of the Roman Empire, the little 'Celtic Churches' are seen as flickering lights of independence at the end of Europe, their spontaneity finally distinguished by the overbearing bureaucrats from the continent.

But these interpretations of the Synod of Whitby are likely to cause bewilderment in Irish, Welsh and Scottish circles. Contrary to the understanding of English proponents, who believe that all other Celtic churches crumbled and adopted the decisions of Whitby, this episode does not figure in their history. The belief that the Synod of Whitby directly influenced the churches in the Celtic-speaking lands may itself be an unwitting example of cultural domination. English writers who assume

this influence also assume that modern political and demo-
graphic relations were the same now as then. However, the Irish
and Welsh of the seventh century are much more likely to have
seen themselves not as peripheral but as culturally superior to
third-generation *arrivistes* from Jutland. For the Irish today, as
members of the European Union, as beneficiaries of it, and in
the main as cultural Catholics, the Synod of Whitby is a non-
event on the neighbouring island.

Conclusions

We have seen that some of the themes relate to what we know
about early Christianity in this part of the world, while others
have at best a tenuous link. Either way, the themes seem to have
developed in recent times to suit our own society and its perceived spiritual needs. Poetry and prose, some ancient, some
more recent, became known in translation to certain gifted writers, and it was felt that they provided a freshness to which
Christians today could relate. The themes emerged as they wrote
about their enjoyment of the sources and how they thought they
could be used again. The books they wrote in their turn became
tools that allowed other writers to make further selections from
the rediscovered texts, or to develop new views about them. The
ancient poems and stories, and more recent religious folk poetry,
were used, often as commentaries about contemporary issues,
and they became the subjects for new poems and prayers.

The themes we have considered developed from the reflections and aspirations of some gifted writers in the late twentieth
century, who sought to share with others their findings and their
reflections on what could be relevant today. Other writers with
limited knowledge of the original cultures, and probably none of
the languages, then picked up their works, and treated them not
as reflections but as resources. In this way the understanding of
the themes snowballed as new writers, seeing the same views
repeated, took them as being true to the original sources rather
than recent reflections upon them. Some of the themes that
emerged were reasonable interpretations of the originals, such as
the use of the Trinity and of three-fold expressions; some have
been further removed from their original contexts but certainly
speak directly to contemporary society, such as the nature poetry;

while other themes are based almost entirely on our expectations today, for example, the role of women.

We have suggested why certain themes emerged at this time and were so important, and these need further consideration. Next we will look at the processes of selection and reuse of the poetry and prose, processes which show how certain expectations of Celtic spirituality grew in our own time. We will then consider the impact of new hymns and liturgy, and the desire to live in community.

CHAPTER FIVE

Poetry, prayer and derivative development: How the canon was created

We now turn to how the modern canon of Celtic Christianity has been formed through a selection of books produced in the 1980s and early 1990s, and then how these works were used in turn by other, more recent writers. We will then consider an author who started from a different perspective, the popular Irish writer on Celtic spirituality, John O'Donohue; and finally some of the recent responses by scholars.

We have already seen how books Allchin, de Waal, and the essays edited by James Mackey (1989), helped other writers to discover the existing anthologies of poetry and prose, sources that had also been discovered independently by David Adam, and we have explored how their reflections on the material they found helped to build up certain themes, which were then developed further by contemporary writers and speakers. These writers influenced each other and then influenced still more writers who, with little access to the translations, and no knowledge of the originals, used these new 'translations' or works 'in the Celtic tradition' to write new reflections and meditations.

Adam's books are seen the authentic voice of one who re-discovered the 'Celtic' and made it available to others. However, he does not claim to reproduce the original material. His works are intended for devotional use, not historical study. They contain prose reflections and his own poems, which were written in the style of the *Carmina Gadelica* and 'updated' for an audience with modern concerns. Three of his books are meditations on early Irish poems: *Saint Patrick's Breastplate* (1987), which uses Meyer's translation and Alexander's versification; *The Pilgrim* (2000), which uses an indirect source we will consider later in this chapter; and *Be thou my Vision* (2001), which uses Hull's translation. He includes in each of these books other devotional literature from a wide range of periods, together with personal anecdotes, all of them intended to illustrate his points. His books are fairly short, attractive, sell well and have had widespread influence. Even scholars like Ian Bradley (1993, 59) sometimes depend on Adam as a source. While he relies on translations, his reading is wide and he sometimes sees a use in sources not taken up by others. An example is his reflection on a ninth-century Irish poem, the Old Woman of Beare's lament for lost youth, translated in Carney's *Medieval Irish Lyrics* (Adam 1994, ix, Carney 1967, 29-41).

De Waal used a wider range of sources than many who followed, and included Charles Plummer's monumental *Lives of the Irish Saints*, a collection of Latin and early Irish texts with translations of the Irish texts. Excerpts she includes in her books are sometimes used by other writers, but it is usually clear that they did not go back to the sources or use anything new from them. De Waal herself, as we have seen, used extracts from other works, such as Waddell's *Beasts and Saints*, which demonstrate how a limited number of stories can be passed around, even within the works of one author. An example is her retelling the tale of a fox who lived in community with other animals, led by Saint Ciaran. One day he ran away with the abbot's shoes, but was brought back by his badger brother and did penance for his lapse. In her 1991 book *A World made Whole* (p 83), this story appears without a reference while in a later book, *The Celtic Way of Prayer* (1996, 155), it appears again, this time with a reference to her re-editing in 1995 of Waddell's *Beasts and Saints* (Waddell 1934, 101-6). While none of these uses means it has been distorted, others have since used her as a source, without going back further to explore works which might enrich modern Celtic spirituality. As we have seen, while Celtic spirituality covers many subjects, it often lacks depth because it is based on a limited number of early texts, and limited interpretations of them.

Another feature of her books is her citing of folk material side by side with prose and poetry from the early medieval period. This practice has been taken up enthusiastically by others who may make little distinction between original texts, some of them many centuries old, and recently-composed poetry, treating them as part of a continuum. De Waal herself sees this as acceptable practice, and argues that texts are connected across the

centuries (1991,129). Other less rigorous writers may jump from
the seventh century to the twentieth without leaving signs they
have done this.

She has worked mainly on the Hebridean folk prayers, using
the early medieval texts as supporting material. Yet, as Donald
Meek points out in his chapter 'Conversion, Conflict and
Continuity' (2000, 195-212), the history of the Hebrides was by
no means static. Massive changes included the coming of the
Vikings, the Reformations, the Clearances and emigration.
Meanwhile, Ireland underwent substantial church restructuring
in the twelfth century, together with much building, and an outpouring of literary expression and revision of its literature.
Wales too underwent an outburst of creativity in the eleventh
and twelfth centuries. In each country there also was massive
political and social change, much of it bloody, causing widespread disruption and the movement of populations and their
possessions, including books and craftwork. Continuity cannot
be taken for granted, and apart from the connecting thread of
the languages we may need to be cautious in attributing the same
experiences or expressions of spirituality across the centuries and
across church belief and practice.

Where a doctrinal matter, like the centrality of the Trinity, is
in question, we would expect to see similarities across time,
though this does not mean that these expressions are part of a
continuing tradition other in that they are found across the
Christian world. The nature poetry may provide some indication of a continuing tradition as de Waal claims, for the medieval
and the Hebridean folk poetry do have aspects in common, a
vividness of expression and an identification of the concrete
aspects of daily life, through life lived out in a very different
fashion. We have seen too that there are questions on whether
Alexander Carmichael's *Carmina Gadelica* always reflects prayers
said by Hebrideans, or whether a certain amount of editing and
joining has gone on.

In addition to the circumstances in which similarities occur
because people in different countries and centuries are drawing
on a common biblical heritage or natural cycle, there are times
when an individual story or poem may have journeyed between
the printed text and the oral tradition and then journeyed back

again. Printed editions have sometimes come into the knowledge of the 'common people', and fed the popular tradition. To demonstrate this, we can take one example that has not become part of Celtic spirituality, and one that has.

The story has already been mentioned of Saint Cannera who requested a burial place on Scattery Island, the monastic home of Saint Senan. In the twelfth-century *Life* of this sixth-century saint, he refused because he did not allow women onto his island. While standing on the sea she had walked across to reach Scattery Island, she retorted with a spirited defence of women, rendered in the stilted English translation by Whitley Stokes in the *Lives of the Saints from the Book of Lismore*: 'Christ is no worse that thou. Christ came to redeem women no less than to redeem men. No less did he suffer for the sake of women than for the sake of men. Women have given service and tendance unto Christ and his apostles. No less than men do women enter the heavenly kingdom. Why, then, shouldst thou not take women to thee in thine island?' He gave her hospitality and a grave below the shoreline, where he thought it would be washed away. (Stokes 1890, 219-20)

This story has been reprinted in some collections, such as Marsh and Bamford's *Anthology of Celtic Christianity* (1986, 76-8), and in other more recent books. A brief oral version of this story was recorded on Scattery Island in the early 1950s while it was still inhabited, and is preserved in Ireland's National Folklore Collection (NFC ms 1358, 349). This excludes the walking on the water, but adds the vivid detail that Senan shook his fist at Cannera while she shouted: 'I'm going to die'. It shortens her riposte to: '"When Our Lord died on the Cross" she said to him, "He died for women as well as men".' The story was not known in oral tradition in Irish as far as we know, but was derived, apparently, from Stokes' translation, though it was told in colloquial west-of-Ireland English. The speaker adds that there is a slab of rock seen at very low tide under which Cannera is said to be buried. A shorter version was recounted in 2008 in Kilrush, which referred to the 'Lady's Grave', a slab visible at low tide which bears this name. This name may owe itself to the ballad by Thomas Moore, 'St Senanus and the Lady', which sits very lightly to the legend indeed.

This is an example of a printed text returning to oral telling, though there is no reason to believe that this story was particularly widespread, or that it had been known for long, or that it influenced people outside of the local culture.

When the story passes beyond the local culture and repertoire, much wider interpretations can be placed on the material by the writer or their audience. How a story is used can be a matter of personal artistic preference, but a problem arises when a new adaptation together with the author's personal understanding, with no clear sense of what is received and what is interpreted, becomes the standard text.

There is a poem attributed to the tenth or eleventh century, printed by Kenneth Jackson, which includes the lines:

I should like to have a great ale-feast for the King of Kings; I should like the Heavenly Host to be drinking it for all eternity.

I should like to have the fruits of Faith, of pure devotion; I should like to have the seats of Repentance in my house.

I should like to have the men of Heaven in my own dwelling; I should like the tubs of Long-Suffering to be at their service.

I should like to have the vessels of Charity to dispense; I should like to have the pitchers of Mercy for their company.

I should like there to be Hospitality for their sake; I should like Jesus to be here always.

I should like to have the Three Marys of glorious renown; I should like to have the Heavenly Host from every side.

I should like to be rent-payer to the Lord; he to whom he gives a good blessing has done well in suffering distress. (Jackson 1971, 284-5).

De Waal in a section on Saint Bridget reproduces a folk version:

An old Kerrywoman in the south-west of Ireland today still recites a poem which may well be in origin as old as the tenth or eleventh century.

I would like to have the men of heaven
In my own house;
With vats of good cheer
Laid out for them.

I would like to have the three Marys,
Their fame so great.
I would like people
From every corner of heaven.

I would like them to be cheerful
In their drinking,
I would like to have Jesus too
Here amongst them.

I would like a great lake of beer
for the King of Kings,
I would like to be watching heaven's family
Drinking it through all eternity. (de Waal 1991, 24-5)

This version was taken, as she states, from the introduction by W. R. Rodgers to the translation of the biography of the noted Blasket Island storyteller Peig Sayers (Sayers 1962, xii). Rodgers, who was not an Irish speaker, does not tell us if there were other verses which contained the references to repentance, suffering and charity, or whether this is the complete folk poem. He did not claim that it had continued in popular tradition, but describes it as 'as homely and intimate today as it was to the Gaelic poet of the Middle Ages'. De Waal expands this hint and creates a continuity by saying it is still recited. However, Peig Sayers died in 1958 and the English translation Rodgers introduces was published in 1962. The old Kerrywoman was presumably a contemporary of Peig, and even if she was alive and still reciting when de Waal was writing, this means only the folk poem had been in circulation for a generation or two. Moreover, de Waal associates the poem with Saint Bridget, while Jackson's understanding in his Notes to the medieval poem is: 'A religious poet imagines himself as a tributary tenant of God, rendering the Irish legal dues of lodging and entertainment to his overlord and his retinue' (Jackson 1971, 323).

The reciter probably heard the medieval text read by one of the early twentieth-century scholars who learnt Irish in the area, and possibly by Jackson himself. As the original Irish would have been incomprehensible to a modern speaker, she is likely to have heard it in English and may never have reworked it into her native language. She found it valuable enough to make her own, and through the work of de Waal and the printed word it has found a new and appreciative audience. From an aesthetic point of view, even in translation, the folk poetry is good in its own right, but it has been used by as a continuation of a thousand-year-old tradition, and associated not with its original imagery of lordship and obligation but with the bounty of Saint Bridget. The role of Bridget as a model of hospitality has been strengthened, but we have lost the range of imagery and resonance that comes from the inculturation of Christianity in early Ireland, the sharing of food, with all its biblical connotations, as expressed though the legal and cultural expectations of the original poem. A modern equivalent, ('The Lord is my tax assessesor') would not convey the direct relationship of tenant and overlord, nor indicate that the desire to provide an abundance that could not always be met, and may often have involved some sacrifice. The loss of connection with this layer of meaning arguably diminishes the poem and limits the insights it could provide for a modern reader.

An oral artist may then occasionally incorporate printed material they find useful and aesthetically pleasing. It is a different matter when a historical text, whether it originated in the same place or not, gets known to and taken up into a living tradition that will adapt it to the wider culture, for a different cultural purpose.

To understand how the texts produced by one writer are then used in turn as original sources, regardless of the author's original intentions, we turn to a well-known writer on popular spirituality. A significant figure in a Christian community at Little Gidding in England, Robert Van de Weyer produced an anthology, *Celtic Fire*, in 1990. This contains translations of extracts from the writings of Bede and his contemporaries and free adaptations of early Irish poems and prose. His writings were influential in the early stages of Celtic Christianity, were taken up by others, and his texts were treated as translations from ancient sources. One of his poems is in fact based on Jackson's translation of the medieval poem on the ale-feast (1990, 20-1).

Van de Weyer's introduction to *Celtic Fire* identifies what to him is the reason that 'the Celtic fire is burning anew', the ecological crisis. He then identifies what he sees as the three main components of Celtic Christianity: ancient druidic religion; the Desert Fathers, who were unsullied by Roman ideas; and the doctrines of the 'great British heretic' Pelagius, who is described as having complained about the lavish lifestyle on the continent, and promulgated a theology of intimacy with the divine. All of these premises are debatable, for we know little of druidic religion except through early Christian medieval commentaries; the Desert Fathers, who certainly influenced early Irish monasticism, saw themselves as part of a universal church; and both what Pelagius believed and the extent of his influence are much debated. These are however the starting-point for this writer, and help to explain his approach.

His purpose is clearly devotional, but because he claims much for it, and because he has influenced other writers and expectations of the 'Celtic', his methodology is significant. Much of the time he does not cite poems and prose sections in full, or give the period in which they were composed, or give an indication of where he has cut them. He sees his collection as culled from 'the widest possible sources and scholarly works', and refers the reader to the page-long bibliography at the end. He also writes that he heard the stories he recounts during his childhood in Ireland, and that he has put different sources and translations side by side 'and made a new version, using modern forms of speech' (1990,12). This is a substantial claim to authenticity, and Van de Weyer explains: 'For the purposes of scholarship this may seem to lack precision; but, since the primary sources are mainly oral, the editor's task must be to convey the spirit of the original piece, rather than pursue literal accuracy.' However, most of the sources Van de Weyer uses were not oral at all but conscious literary creations in Old Irish which had been printed in scholarly editions. If the family retainers of his youth really were able to recite them as he claims, they must have been reading learned journals such as *Ériu* and *Zeitschrift für Celtische Philologie*. This is unlikely though, as we have seen, not impossible; and the literary origins of his Irish material are clear through the notes contained in the later anthologies he uses, the main one of which is Murphy's *Early Irish Lyrics*, published in 1956 and referred to in his bibliography. While Marsh and Bamford in their anthology took existing translations of Irish, Welsh and English texts, Van de Weyer has created his own.

Some of his material has sunk without further influence. He used the prose translation by Murphy of the poem that has been versified as 'Be thou my vision', to make his own version, under the title 'Lord of my heart' (1990, 93-4). The hymn version had established itself well enough in church life and modern Celtic spirituality to retain its place.

Some of Van de Weyer's renderings remain relatively close to Murphy's English translations, but some deviate considerably. This is the case with 'Two hermits in one house' (1990, 69-70), which is based very loosely upon a well-known poem published by Meyer, believed to be of the eleventh century, which is attributed to a known writer, Máel Ísu Úa Brolcháin (d. 1086), a member of the abbatial family from Derry. In this much-discussed poem a monk addresses 'Crinóg', 'Old-Young', speaking as to a woman and in terms of courtly love. The scholar James Carney took the view, which has been generally accepted since, that it is in fact addressed not to a woman but to a psalter. Translated in prose in Greene and O'Connor's anthology *A Golden Treasury of Early Irish Poetry* (1967), this was also one of the poems that Frank O'Connor versified and it turns up, accompanied by this interpretation, in various Irish anthologies. Indeed in mid-twentieth-century Ireland, it is difficult to see how a poem placed in the mouth of a monk and addressed to the Lady Old-Young, with whom he has slept, and who has slept with others, would otherwise have got past the censors.

> Though when at first we went to bed,
> Sweet girl whose wisdom comes from heaven,
> I was a boy with no bad thoughts,
> A modest lad, and barely seven. (O'Connor 1959, 367)

In Van de Weyer's version it starts the same but the other expectations of hermits then take over.

> You slept with four men after that,
> Yet did not sin in leaving me,

And now a virgin you come back –
I see the thing that all men see. (O'Connor 1959, 367)

becomes:

When we were married we lived a simple, blameless life, working hard during the day and enjoying one another at night …
You bore five children and I toiled in the fields to feed them …

While not widely disseminated, this poem may have helped
to develop the view, further popularised by Peter Tremayne in
his Sister Fidelma novels, that married religious life was the
norm in the early churches on these islands, even, it seems,
among hermits.

Van de Weyer's 'Brendan's Prayer on the mountain' (1990,
30) shows how material can be adapted and then influence
others. His poem comes after a section in *Celtic Fire* based upon
the prose voyage of Saint Brendan, and fits well with the movement's interest in pilgrimage, and the journey to the edges. The
source for Van de Weyer's version is the poem published as 'The
Pilgrim' by Greene and O'Connor (1967, 151-3), which is based
on an edition of the single surviving manuscript by Kuno Meyer
in *Zeitschrift für Celtische Philologie* (x, 1909, 45-47). The original
poem is attributed by Meyer to the scholarly king of Munster,
Cormac Mac Cuileannáin who died in 903, though Greene and
O'Connor thought it was later. In the poem, the wealthy speaker
asks himself if he should leave the comforts of life for the poverty of pilgrimage across the sea and the hardships it imposes
through confession, penance and physical danger. It opens in
Greene and O'Connor's translation:

Shall I go, O King of the Mysteries, after my fill of cushions
and music, to turn my face on the shore and my back on my
native land?

Van de Weyer has:
Shall I abandon, O king of Mysteries, the soft comforts of
home? Shall I turn my back on my native land and my face
towards the sea?

Greene and O'Connor:
Shall I say a long farewell to the great island of the sons of
Mil?

Van de Weyer:
Shall I say farewell to my beautiful land ...

Greene and O'Connor:
Shall I take my little black curragh over the broad-breasted, glorious ocean? O King of the bright kingdom, shall I go of my own choice upon the sea?

Van de Weyer:
Shall I take my tiny coracle across the wide, sparkling ocean? O King of the Glorious Heaven, shall I go of my own choice upon the sea?

Greene and O'Connor:
Whether I be strong or poor, or mettlesome so as to be re-counted in tales, O Christ, will you help me when it comes to going upon the wild sea?

Van de Weyer has solely:
O Christ, will you help me on the wild waves?

The poem is not the work of the ascetic monk Brendan who set sail, if ever, in the sixth century, in search of hermitage or the Land of Promise itself, whose stories are entangled in the litera-ture with journeys to the land of the undying, the pre-Christian otherworld untouched by original sin, death or corruption. It is more likely to refer to the royal pilgrimages to Rome of later centuries. The text was used by other writers before Van de Weyer, including in a romantic passage in Leslie Hardinge's study of early Christianity in Britain (1972,14-15), and the nature imagery of the Irish poem is familiar to us through collections like Jackson's *A Celtic Miscellany*. The battle images are not what we might expect of an ascetic saint like Brendan, but are the product of a warrior society, and potentially moving as such, another example of inculturated Christianity. A parallel might be the imagery in the Old English *Dream of the Rood*, in which Christ is portrayed as a warrior, mounting the cross as an act of courage in the face of his enemies. Van de Weyer's adaptations lack the strangeness of the original imagery to a modern audi-ence, and they also lack the power.

David Adam knew through Hardinge part of the translation by Greene and O'Connor, and gave an excerpt in one of his earlier books, *The Cry of the Deer* (1987, 113-4). However his full-length meditation, *A Desert in the Ocean* (2000), uses Van de Weyer's version, and does not refer to the original translation. While Adam does not always tell us where he has got his material, he usually draws on what he considers genuine, so it seems he considered Van de Weyer's version as valid as the translations of Meyer and Hull which he used for his other full-length meditations.

The widely-read collection, *Celtic Daily Prayer*, published by the Northumbria Community, includes a long meditation on Saint Brendan which is woven around Van de Weyer's version of the medieval Irish poem. Other writers who treat Van de Weyer's version as original include Michael Mitton, who wrote on Celtic spirituality in the interests of renewal and healing from an evangelical perspective (1995, 164-5); and Roger Ellis and Chris Seaton who explored the use of 'Celtic' themes for church renewal in *New Celts* (1998, 178). A shortened version, 'A Pilgrim's Plea, attributed to St Brendan', with a reference to Van de Weyer, is printed in the 'Celtic Christianity' section of Michael Counsell's *2000 Years of Prayer*, among other shortened pieces (1999, 73-4).

Greene and O'Connor's 1967 anthology was reprinted in 1990, but this powerful twelfth-century poem has been replaced in popular Celtic spirituality by Van de Weyer's adaptation, which is now associated with Saint Brendan, one of the movement's thematic saints.

This demonstrates one of the weaknesses of movement, how a loss of depth, historical, literary and spiritual, is caused by relying on derivative creations. The original poetry is still appreciated in a different milieu. Greene and O'Connor's text was sung in modernised Irish as part of Shaun Davey's composition *The Pilgrim* (1983, 1992). This was intended for a secular audience interested in music from all the Celtic countries. It is arguably truer to the original.

Van de Weyer is not alone in making changes and in leaving few markers and, like most of his contemporaries, saw his role as producing moving spiritual resources rather than academic works. He makes this explicit in a later book, *Celtic Gifts* (1997) which suggests ways in which his Anglican Church could adopt the early saints as inspiration for mission.

As we have seen, Adam makes no claim that his poems are translations, and a reader of Van de Weyer's *Celtic Daily Prayer* might realise from other excepts that they are not direct translations, even if there is no indication of where to find them. But other writers have used them without being aware of the sources. Some, like Ellis and Seaton (1998) were conscious that they were using 'Celtic' as a metaphor, and that their material was derived from like-minded people, and that their purpose, resourcing church renewal, justified this approach.

Treating collections or commentaries as real sources makes certain works more widely known, but it has meant too that the richness of the originals and an understanding of the cultures that produced them, has been lost, leaving the 'Celtic' increasingly self-derivative. The intention was to make material accessible rather than to narrow it, and collections like *Celtic Fire* may have been used so eagerly because they seemed useful. In turn, writings like *Celtic Fire* were validated by being cited. Then, when a writer like David Adam, who is a recognised poet, comments on Celtic spirituality, whether he wishes it or not, he is regarded as an authority.

Another influential work already mentioned is *Celtic Daily Prayer*, which contains both 'Celtic' themes and prose and poetry selected from all periods and places. This was compiled by the Northumbria Community, an ecumenical Christian community founded at the time when Celtic spirituality was developing. Membership is dispersed but it has premises in north-east England where courses and retreats are run, and is to some respects similar to the Iona Community. The men who founded it are known as writers and speakers on Celtic spirituality, and it has forged a distinctive role in two areas, the production of popular liturgies, especially those in the 'Celtic tradition', and much less well-known bereavement support and help for those who have suffered in the churches.

Celtic Daily Prayer is a composite work, recently republished in paperback (2005), which is based on several earlier editions intended for use at the traditional offices of Morning and Evening Prayer. The current volume includes liturgies, short biographies of traditional saints and recently deceased people for assigned daily reflection; longer meditations, including one based on the Byrne-Hull hymn 'Be thou my vision' (2005, 597-615); and two cycles of daily prayer named respectively after Saints Aidan and Finan. Most of the prayers are taken from contemporary but not widely-known writers, but excerpts thought to be from prayers in the Celtic languages, whether ancient or modern, are also included.

This is a devotional work, intended for both communal and individual use. One of the longer pieces, intended for private meditation, is on the voyages of Saint Brendan, and starts with a poem based on Van de Weyer's paraphrase of the Irish pilgrimage poem (2005, 184-99). The reader is recommended to read Tim Severin's *The Brendan Voyage*, a book based on a journey across the Atlantic in a modern currach, and neither Van de Weyer nor Hardinge nor Carney are cited. This meditation also uses images taken from the old English poems *The Seafarer* and *The Wanderer*. Elsewhere, *Celtic Daily Prayer* uses, again without naming its source, part the hymn found in the Catholic Morning and Evening Prayer designated for Wednesday evenings in Week Two, 'I walk the lonely mountain road' (2005, 482). This hymn is itself based on a medieval Irish poem edited and translated by Carney (1967, 42-7), and as we have seen is one of several in the Catholic Office which have themselves been silently derived from Irish anthologies. In *Celtic Daily Prayer* it is attributed to Saint Columba. It is notable, though, that none of the writings actually attributed to this saint by his successors are used at all, possibly because they are too strong for this popular and engaging collection, and possibly because it had taken shape before the 1995 edition of these poems by Markús and Clancy. Other writers, like Peter Millar of the Iona Community (1998, 93), have followed *Celtic Daily Prayer* or one of its earlier incarnations in attributing this prayer to Saint Columba.

In common with much of the current movement, this compilation is Protestant in tone but places great emphasis on the lives of the saints. They are sometimes addressed directly in prayers, but in the meditations they are presented as models. The Virgin Mary is given a briefer biography than many other saints, and she is not made a focus of devotion. Most of the saints mentioned are from early Christian Northumbria, but the biographies also cover a number of Irish female saints, and Pelagius

(c. 350-418), John Wycliffe (1324-84), the late medieval translator of the Bible into English, and the American civil rights activist Martin Luther King (1929-68). The same eclectic coverage of is found in the prayers and meditations, which are taken from the church Fathers, folk prayers, works of English literature, modern Celtic compositions such as 'Caim' (encircling) prayers 'for when I do not know what to pray' (2005, 305-6), and other modern poetry. A verse taken from the Derry singer Phil Coulter's, 'A town I loved so well' is followed by some lines from T. S. Eliot's *Four Quartets* (2005, 442). *Celtic Daily Prayer* seems to have grown out of the contributions of many different people, and 'what worked' verbally and suited a particular theme, has been incorporated into the text.

As a devotional collection many of the contents would stand alone, but by naming it *Celtic Daily Prayer* it is suitable for the Community, provides something readers will identify with, and gains a certain authority. The current understanding of 'Celtic' allows this wide variety of material to be gathered together and made into something workable today. The Celtic badge certainly works, for *Celtic Daily Prayer* is not vastly different from similar collections, including the many published by Wild Goose Publications, but is referred to by many users as an aid to prayer. As such, it is arguably fulfilling the purpose for which it was intended.

Given the limited use of the original sources and their languages, it is not surprising that some of the people who spearheaded Celtic spirituality have been defensive over their selection of what is Celtic. A founder of the Northumbria Community warned participants at one talk of the 'academic temptation' of seeking for historical interpretations rather than accepting Celtic spirituality as something to be experienced.[1] The website and publications of the Community of Aidan and Hilda also express reservations about an academic approach, which suggests that they had experienced criticism. It declares:

> Two common pitfalls to avoid are: Academic study that divorces intellectual analysis from the living of life. The great church teachers of early centuries lived what they thought.

---

1. Talk at Swanwick Conference Centre by Roy Searle, Derbyshire, 20 May 1996.

They united obedience to truth with thinking about truth. Western universities lost this holistic approach. We seek to restore through the heart study ...

University courses: If you have the time, money, aptitude and motivation to undertake accredited university courses you could find out from the internet about the courses at the universities of Wales, Cork, Edinburgh and Cambridge. However, note the first warning above. (www.aidanandhilda.org.uk (accessed 13/01/10)

This approach suggests that exploring the originals does not have the same priority as applying them, and it is notable that the instigators of the English version of Celtic spirituality, such as Van de Weyer, Adam, Ray Simpson and the founders of the Northumbria Community, have spent some twenty years on the Celtic but none has so far published fresh translations from the original languages.

One of the reasons for the development of *Celtic Daily Prayer* and a similar but less well-known compilation by the Community of Aidan and Hilda was the impact in the 1980s of the liturgies and hymns of the oldest 'Celtic' Community, the Iona Community. The origins of this community will be discussed in the next chapter, but we can turn briefly to the development of liturgies designed primarily for use in worship in Iona Abbey. These originated in the 1940s and 1950s when they were produced annually, printed as leaflets and sold to visitors. It was only with the publication of the first *Iona Community Worship Book* in 1988, that 'Celtic' themes and language became dominant. A second version of this book, known as the *Grey Worship Book,* was produced in 1991 when one of the key writers on Celtic spirituality, Philip Newell, was Warden of the Abbey. The earlier book, which was known from its cover as the *Black Worship Book,* had a punchy social approach, but the version overseen by Newell is much gentler, has a vocabulary and cadences more like those of Carmichael's *Carmina Gadelica* translations, and contained among other innovations a 'Celtic Evening Liturgy'. These books are used far beyond Iona, the style has been widely copied, and the impact on church services has been considerable.

These liturgies, especially the second one, used the same practice as the Northumbria Community in gathering material from a range of sources and setting them together without comment. To take one example, the *Grey Worship Book* contains a prayer:

Deep peace of the running wave to you,
Deep peace of the flowing air to you,
Deep peace of the quiet earth to you,
Deep peace of the shining stars to you,
Deep peace of the Son of Peace to you.

This is sometimes set to music, including music composed by the Iona Community's Wild Goose Worship Group, and is usually credited with being an anonymous 'ancient Celtic blessing'.

The original was composed by William Sharp, writing as Fiona MacLeod, whom the *Grey Worship Book* notes as the author (1991, 58, 63). It was derived from a longer poem, 'Invocation of Peace', which appears in the posthumous collection *From the Hills of Dream* (MacLeod [Sharp] 1907), the whole of which was reprinted in a volume by Marian McNeill published in 1947 by the Iona Community as *An Iona Anthology*. A revised version of this volume, which contains several extracts from Fiona MacLeod's writings, appeared in 1952. At some stage, a number of lines from this poem were selected and adapted from a section which originally read:

Deep peace of the running wave to you,
Deep peace of the flowing air to you,
Deep peace of the quiet earth to you,
Deep peace of the sleeping stones to you!
Deep peace of the Yellow Shepherd to you,
Deep peace of the Wandering Shepherdess to you,
Deep peace of the Flock of Stars to you,
Deep peace from the Son of Peace to you,
Deep peace from the heart of Mary to you,
From Bridget of the Mantle
Deep peace, deep peace!

The flock of stars have been changed to shining stars, the peace from the Son of Peace has been slightly modified, and the

sleeping stones, Yellow Shepherd and the Wandering Shepherdess have vanished altogether. So has Sharp/MacLeod's claim
that this poem was from the Gaelic of an 'Alan Dall', Blind Alan.
(MacLeod 1907, 26, McNeill 1952, 58–9.) The references to Mary
and Bridget, have not been used, nor have the final lines of the
poem, which demonstrate how MacLeod had moved towards
Christianity. It continues:

> And with the kindness too of the Haughty Father,
> Peace!
> In the name of the Three who are One,
> And by the will of the King of the Elements,
> Peace! Peace!

The verse in its current form is found in many Pagan and
Christian books and websites. They can be as diverse as the
Baptist Union of Great Britain's *Worship Book* where it appears
as part of the Funeral Liturgy's 'Act of Committal' (1991, 141), or
the Pagan versions that change the invocation to the 'Son of
Peace' to something more in tune with pantheism.

The original poem was still known in some places, for the
Corrymeela Community uses the Iona Community form but
first gives the preceding five lines from Sharp's poem:

> Deep peace, pure white of the moon to you
> Deep peace, pure green of the grass to you
> Deep peace, pure brown of the earth to you
> Deep peace, pure grey of the dew to you
> Deep peace, pure blue of the sky to you. (Hamill, 2001, 95)

The latest *Iona Abbey Worship Book* (2001) accepts the existence of Celtic spirituality, if not necessarily all aspects of the
movement. The liturgies were supplemented by the *Wee Worship
Book* series produced in the late 1980s and 1990s by the liturgists
and hymnodists John Bell and Graham Maule. They again use
language modelled on the *Carmina Gadelica* translations, but
have a strong emphasis on social justice and international affairs, matters that on the whole have not been taken up into
modern Celtic spirituality.

So far we have considered English and Scottish works. It was
suggested earlier that the Irish form of Celtic spirituality is in

part a reaction to the use by others of the native heritage. It transpired to be just as wide-ranging when it did take off, though
the range is different, as can be seen in the works of John
O'Donohue (1956-2007), a native Irish speaker, who like David
Adam, had a considerable personal following. His works show
a new development in the understanding of Celtic, and so far
have not been copied or used as original resources.

His first book on this subject *Anam Cara: Spiritual Wisdom
from the Celtic World*, published in 1997, was produced for both a
home and a Celtic spirituality market. The title words for 'soul
friend' would be recognised by followers of Celtic spirituality in
Britain, and while the term was not a familiar one in Ireland,
both words would have been known to those educated in
schools in the Republic, while any uncertainty for either audience is cleared up by the subtitle. He introduces his view of the
Celtic in a form people familiar with the movement would
recognise, and those who were not could relate to, by declaring
in a manner reminiscent of the last Celtic Twilight:

> The Celtic mind was neither discursive nor systematic. Yet in
> their lyrical speculation, the Celts brought the sublime unity
> of life and experience to expression. The Celtic mind was not
> burdened by dualism. It did not separate what belongs together.
> The Celtic imagination articulated the inner friendship which
> embraces nature, divinity, underworld and human world as
> one. The dualism which separates the visible from the invisible,
> time from eternity, the human from the divine, was totally
> alien to them. Their sense of ontological friendship yielded a
> world of experience imbued with a rich texture of otherness,
> ambivalence, symbolism and imagination. For our sore and
> tormented separation, the possibility of this imaginative and
> unifying friendship is the Celtic gift.

Whether we accept or understand this or not, including the
use of 'ontological', the rich texture of his sentences help to give
a sense that what follows will be worth the effort. He goes on to
explain his purpose as: 'In essence this book attempts a phe-
nomenology of friendship in a lyrical-speculative form'(1997,
18-19).

While much of his style and content may seem impenetrable,

his books were an instant success in Ireland and in America, and gained a following in Britain. His ability to combine theologically complex ideas and specialised vocabulary with everyday subjects, usually in sections of about 350 words, means that his writings are ideal for regular personal or group reflection. An expert on the medieval spiritual writer, Meister Eckhart, O'Donohue also knew the printed folk collections of twentieth-century Ireland, and the surviving oral traditions of the west where he lived, and he weaved them effectively into his reflections. *Anam Cara* was followed by other books in the same mould, which show evidence of wide spiritual reading and are sprinkled with sayings from Irish. Even the ways the books were produced were designed to resonate with our expectations of the spiritual and the special, for the original hardback versions are similar to the presentation missals and bibles designed for First Communion and Confirmation. They have paper covers and a ribbon to mark the place, and are printed on thick parchment-like paper with titles and subheadings in a variation of Celtic script. The title-page of his *Anam Cara* has a dot over the 'C', which in Gaelic script denotes the sound change now normally written 'Ch'. The Irish audience would recognise the Gaelic script, used by civil servants until the mid-twentieth-century, and it provides a sense of the book being embedded in the native heritage, authenticating its 'Celtic' nature. However, a knowledge of Irish is not necessary, which makes the books accessible to most people in Ireland as well as to a market abroad. His works, including his last two, a bilingual collection of poetry (2000) and a book of blessings (2007), are published with co-ordinating pastel covers. They are widely read and O'Donohue proved to one of the most popular speakers ever at England's annual liberal-evangelical Christian Arts Festival, Greenbelt.

O'Donohue presented his material as a reflection on a remaining, little-known but still vibrant native culture. His view of the 'Celtic' was certainly influenced by local traditions in a way the English, and even the Welsh and Scottish are not, and unlike the English version where the Celtic is something to be rediscovered and reclaimed, he saw himself and other like-minded people as working from within a native culture which has never died. Like Seán Ó Duinn he treated the Scots Gaelic

Carmina Gadelica as part of his own tradition, as part of this cultural continuum that existed over time and indeed place. We can see this at work in a section of *Anam Cara* concerning death, where a prayer from the *Carmina Gadelica* is quoted with Carmichael named as the translator but no indication of where it comes from. It is followed directly by reference to contemporary Conamara tradition (O'Donohue 1997, 250-1).

His understanding of the desires of the movement to find new means of expression of faith, and his ability to convey this poetically can be seen in an extract from his second book, *Eternal echoes*, on 'the prison of belief':

> The Wildness of Celtic spirituality
> The world of Celtic spirituality never had such walls. It was not a world of clear boundaries; people and things were never placed in bleak isolation from each other; everything was connected and there was a sense of the pliant flow of presences in and out of each other. The physical world was experienced as the structure of an invisible world which flowed underneath it and whose music reverberated upon us ... The Celtic universe was the homeland of the inspirational and the unexpected ... Part of the wisdom of the Celtic imagination was the tendency to keep realities free and fluent ... They saw themselves as guests in a living, breathing universe. (1998, 117-8.)

Many other writers could relate to this, though it is some way from the views of Adam, or Ellis and Seaton on the 'Celtic' as a tool for church development, and many might struggle with the section that directly follows, which concerns the fairies. This is a very long way from writers like the English evangelical Michael Mitton, who feared in *Restoring the Woven Cord* that some of the poems of the *Carmina Gadelica* were occult (1995, 173).

O'Donohue's range is as wide as that of the other leading writers on Celtic spirituality, though his choice of reading is different. In the opening pages of his 2003 book *Divine Beauty*, he cites in rapid succession the twentieth-century theologian Hans Urs von Balthasar, the Irish politician Michael D. Higgins, another twentieth-century theologian Hans-Georg Gadamer, the poet Kathleen Raine, Saint Augustine of Hippo, the medieval

Meister Eckhart, and various lesser-known people. He connects ideas across time and place in a series of personal reflections that have a wider appeal. The books give a sense of intimacy as he draws from his personal experience of family life and an appreciation of traditional rural society. His prose soothes the reader into a sense of comfort which enables us to accept the learnedness without needing to enquire further. Even so, it has a sameness similar to that of many works of the Celtic Twilight, and while many enjoy his books, it is possible that they are more often dipped into than read from cover to cover.

The success of O'Donohue's writing is partly due to his mellifluous style, his ability to write in sections, and his all-encompassing, compassionate approach to issues. They must also owe much to his circumstances and the time at which the books appeared. A former priest living as a hermit, he started publishing at a time of backlash against the Catholic Church in Ireland and in North America. This came after a series of cases became public where priests had abused children, and the Catholic hierarchy had failed to act, or as later transpired, had engaged in cover-ups. His books, the first of which went into eleven reprints in two years, offered an alternative, apparently native, deeper, older, purer spirituality at a time when the sense of institutional betrayal by the Catholic Church was high. As O'Donohue had left the priesthood, he was free from being associated with the institution, and his circumstances may have appealed to readers who were on the point of leaving church life but did not want to leave Christianity. His later books sold less well, perhaps because of the repetitive format and possibly because that particular bout of anger ran its course. The change in focus in his last two books, followed by his sudden death, may reverse this trend. Another factor may be that the anger with the Catholic Church has returned in Ireland, but on a still greater scale in consequence of two official reports published in 2009 on institutional abuse by Catholic religious organisations and by clergy of the Archdiocese of Dublin. The consequences of these revelations and the scale of cover-up have social consequences which are only beginning to be understood. With an increasing chasm between spiritual practice and traditional church attendance, O'Donohue's works may yet last.

The academic response

Another kind of backlash, though a much less public one, has been led by academics concerned at the way that Celtic spirituality takes material out of context and attributes to it matters that are to do with twentieth-century interests and expectations rather than with the original sources. This is in part about tensions between the popular use of texts for religious ends and their study for intellectual ones, and there may be an element in the scholarly response of resistance to the harvesting of the fruits of their subject to use for an ulterior purpose. For many scholars their subject is an affair of the heart as well as the head and most reactions are not in response to the use for devotional purposes but to what is seen as misuse or misinterpretation of the sources.

As we have seen there is considerable debate concerning the existence of Celtic Christianity at all. Most academics point out that in many cases we know very little about the original uses of the material, or that it has been distorted by reinterpretations over time, and that many essential aspects of the ancient and folk tradition have been discarded.

We have seen that Celtic spirituality has little in common with what is taught in universities as Celtic Studies, though there have been some, like the University of Wales at Lampeter which treats it as a separate, but valid, course of study, and offers a Master's degree in Celtic Spirituality. We have seen too that popular views have become so established that scholars have felt it necessary to address them in introductions to otherwise specialised works.

A number of academics, mainly from backgrounds in theology or religious studies, have written about modern Celtic spirituality. Much of their commentary has a certain ambiguity in its approach as the majority are themselves sympathetic to Christianity, and most make suggestions on alternative uses for 'Celtic' material.

The scholars who have responded fall more or less into three groups. The first consists of those who know the original material because they work in the academic disciplines that study it, history, literature, theology, folklore, and in some cases art. Their approach seeks to combine scholarly rigour and reputation with the desire to share the products of their studies in the context of their faith.

An example of this approach is Donald Meek, who combines these tensions with that of being a native Gaelic Islander. A former Professor of Celtic at Edinburgh University, his main contribution, *The Quest for Celtic Christianity* (2000) is learned and entertaining, and though the content is dense it is written in an accessible style, and intended for both a popular and scholarly readership. It is the best reference work to date on modern Celtic spirituality, and gives especial attention to the English form and its use of Scottish material. There is a withering critique of the lack of academic rigour applied by writers on modern Celtic spirituality, and the high level of 'secondary derivation' of books that cite the books of others who are not conversant with any original sources. The level of repetition, he argues, leads to a degree of constriction which is not met by reading the sources or by depth of study, but rather by applying modern Celtic Christianity to an ever-wider range of options and by making increasing claims about what it has to teach the modern audience. (2000, 234). Writing from a Gaelic perspective, he views the movement as consumerist, a harvesting of choice titbits of his culture without considering the wider context or how these pieces grew and are loved by his own society. He urges a return to use of the sources and points to much that he believes could be understood and appreciated on its own terms, including saints, churches, theology, art and literature. (2000, 237-8). He also questions whether the churches of the period before 1100 are the best models for contemporary challenges, given the changes that have occurred across the centuries. An evangelical Baptist, Meek combines knowledge of early Irish and Welsh literature, Gaelic folk tradition, the historiography of the movement, and his personal beliefs and experience, with considerable passion.

Another scholar, Thomas O'Loughlin, addressed the different audiences by writing two books, one as a theologian and historian (2000a) and the other as a contributor to the current movement. His popular account, *Journey on the Edges* (2000b) accepts that people believe there is a Celtic spirituality, and are attracted to the liminality, the 'wildness' that imbues it, and he therefore attempts to ground it by offering in a popular format translations of ancient material and commentaries on the early

Christian Irish way of life. Another Irish scholar, John Carey, takes a similar approach in two seminal works, *A Single Ray of the Sun* (1999), and *King of Mysteries* (2000). O'Loughlin's later book, *Discovering Saint Patrick* (2005) contributes to the movement while attempting to steer it by providing, like Carey, early medieval texts together with an introduction intended for the general as well as an academic reader; taking as given the understanding that many readers will be familiar with modern Celtic spirituality.

Some writers have debunked the excesses of the movement without directly challenging it. Richard Sharpe's translation of Adamnán's *Life of Saint Columba* (1991) provides the background to understanding the text, while another who writes from both a scholarly and Christian perspective is Paul Cavill, whose *Anglo-Saxon Christianity* (1999) does not directly confront the movement but provides information from which it can be assessed.

We have not considered the use of art, but an example of one of those who does, and who shows hints of both Christian discourse and mainstream scholarly approaches is Janet Blackhouse, former curator at the British Library, who has brought the *Lindisfarne Gospels*, written in about 700 AD, to a wider public through books, videos and DVDs. She makes clear that the Lindisfarne and similar gospel books she works on are the products of Anglo-Saxon Christianity. As a scholar she provides the background to understand them as products of their time but in terms that relate to the interests of followers of the current Celtic movement.

A second group of academics write both out of interest in this subject and out of a personal faith, but their professional expertise is in a different field. The fact that they often hold academic posts and write in an academic style inevitably leads them to being regarded as experts in Celtic Christianity. Examples are James Mackey (1989), Donald Allchin (1986, 1993), Esther de Waal (1986, 1989, 1991) and Ian Bradley (1993, 1996, 1999, 2000). The issues for such writers is the extent to which they are able to interpret the sources they use through comparison with the subjects they know in depth; whether their interpretative skills can be transferred to a new area of study; and the impact that the combination of a limited knowledge of the texts and a committed faith have on their audience. In practice, whether they willed it or not, they have become creators of modern Celtic Christianity rather than interpreters of existing belief and practice.

A third group are scholars who have made modern Celtic spirituality their study. Seán Ó Duinn (2000), Oliver Davies (1996), Mary Low (1996) and Mark Atherton (2002) approach the subject from this perspective. Davies wrote on the medieval Welsh spiritual tradition while developing Celtic spirituality as part of the academic world though work at the University of Wales. His approach is to take Celtic Christianity at face value by supplying a selection of the key Welsh texts in new translations with a commentary which gives an historical and theological context. The work is supplemented with a wider anthology of the Welsh medieval texts (Davis and Bowie 1995).

Low wrote as a supporter of the movement and provides material for it in *Celtic Christianity and Nature* (1996). This contains insights for mainstream Celtic Studies scholars, for she uses a combination of works in the original languages and scriptural texts. However, her acceptance of the movement at face value also limits her work, and at times she seems to justify her sources from the perspective of what she already believes to be true. She is writing at least as much for followers of Celtic spirituality as for fellow-academics, and for a society that has complete access to the scriptures. It must be questioned whether the biblical texts she cites were known widely among members of the early churches in the Celtic countries. Her work covers a wide range of early mythology, medieval religious writing and folk practice, though the critical apparatus is not always apparent.

A very different approach was taken by Low's Edinburgh contemporary Gilbert Markús, who jointly produced with Thomas Clancy as evidence of the 'real' Celtic material *Iona: the earliest poetry* (1995), an edition and translation of poetry from the Iona *scriptorium*. This much-needed edition is interspersed with editorial notes and commentaries, which are frequently hostile to modern Celtic spirituality. While these might have been appropriate in a separate article, these asides are inclined to undermine the value of the edition, for it can be hard to see where the editorial voice ends and the personal begins, and many of the comments may bewilder readers in a few years' time. The editors may at times overstate their case, but their translations made a new range of texts available to readers. Clancy went on to edit a collection of papers on Saint Columba in a more mainstream style, while Markús wrote a number popular articles in the Dominican periodical *Spirituality* and elsewhere, with titles such as 'Celtic Schmeltic', arguing against the modern Celtic romantics.

As well as academics writing on other subjects but who find it necessary to comment on it, there are writers with academic credibility who are in some sense involved in the movement and seek to guide it into a more grounded relationship with original sources and the contexts in which they were produced. This leads to a tension, for the writer as well as the audience, over what is presented and how. Which books can be regarded as academic discourses and which are products of the popular movement is not always clear. We can see this with Ian Bradley, for in his first two 'Celtic' books he enthusiastically embraced the movement, in the third, influenced by Donald Meek, he rescinded much of what he had written, and he then returned to the subject in a fourth book to indicate what he thought was genuine and valuable for an audience today. All four of his books continue to be quoted, so his retractions may not have proved effective.

It must also be acknowledged that these scholars have so far had limited influence on the popular movement. It has a life of its own and more bridges may be needed.

Conclusions

We have seen that there is a complex relationship between academic and popular Celtic Christianity. Much of what passes as 'Celtic' is undoubtedly a modern growth for modern needs. However, whatever its roots, the 'Celtic' has a robustness of its own and has been accepted by a wide range of people for what it can offer today.

There are certainly a number of paradoxes. Writers like Adam and Van de Weyer seem to have devised their material for regular worshippers, comfortable with church structures and open to welcoming newcomers introduced to church life through an extended programme of mission and renewal. However, it must be asked whether many people who come to

Christianity will be fed for long on their material, or whether they require something meatier. Starting from another perspective, the Iona Community's liturgies and hymns have been described as liberating and life-giving by people dismayed by traditional churches with declining, ageing populations, denominational wrangling over reorganisation and bitter theological disagreements in public. They may appeal more directly to people whose faith life has developed to a more critical stage which includes individual questioning and a commitment to social activism. O'Donohue's writings may also be aimed more at those exploring their faith in this more critical manner, for they presuppose a familiarity with Christian precepts and a desire to explore apparent inconsistencies.

One matter to consider further in Chapter Seven is whether the popular writers on the Celtic have limited the spirituality of readers by failing to use scholarly texts and interpretations and signposts to the original sources. We may also consider whether some of the original writings from the early Christian churches in Ireland and Britain, jarring though some of them might be, would provide richer resources, and whether even those parts of tradition which cannot be digested should be referred to because they might be relevant to future generations.

Some of the poems, liturgies, hymnody and talks on Celtic spirituality have shown themselves to be very attractive not only to regular churchgoers but to people on the fringes. This can be seen by their use at festivals like Greenbelt and in other non-traditional settings. So in considering its influence it is necessary to ask from a theological perspective whether claims that are factually wrong can still inspire individuals and be theologically right as a path to the divine.

The next chapter will develop this question by looking more fully at one of the key elements of the movement, the emphasis on community, and will explore it through the oldest of the current communities with 'Celtic' attributes. This exploration may help to unlock one of the paradoxes. Much of what was produced was intended to improve devotional and liturgical life and to make the church more attractive to people beyond it; but many of the users are physically or psychologically on the point of leaving church life.

CHAPTER SIX:

Creating Celtic community:
The Iona story

One of the most evident features of the Celtic movement is the interest in community. Sometimes it comes together with the theme of pilgrimage. This chapter looks at the development of the Iona Community, and how it has contributed to modern Celtic spirituality; and then briefly at other communities with a 'Celtic' theme and how they use it.

The Iona Community is older than the contemporary movement, and was not created to promote the 'Celtic'. Even so, it is extremely important in understanding modern Celtic spirituality, because many of the images, liturgies and hymns now used come from it, and have helped the modern understanding of the 'Celtic' to develop. In addition, the Community's recognised but fringe position in Scottish church life helped its popular identification with the 'Celtic' as being 'on the edge' and testing the limits. This has in turn helped the Celtic to become accepted in the churches.

When we consider how the Community started and grew, the kind of people it attracted and its association with a place of ancient pilgrimage, we can see how various themes and material were used to provide for spiritual needs of their time, and how they provided a springboard for Celtic spirituality to develop two generations later. As with certain artistic and musical developments, material appeared in popular form that seemed to address a need, and in the hands of a craftsman like the founder of the Iona Community, something new was shaped.

The Iona Community originally had little in common with what we would expect. It was founded in 1938 by George MacLeod (1895-1991), a Church of Scotland minister who had been a solider in the First World War. He worked in Govan, the shipbuilding area of Glasgow, and saw at first hand the misery caused by the poverty of the Depression. A socialist from a wealthy background, he became a pacifist, at least in part because of his experiences in the trenches. MacLeod was acutely aware that the churches appeared to have nothing to say to the people among whom he worked. He had himself been powerfully influenced by experience of Greek Orthodox liturgy, and believed that the extempore style of Church of Scotland services current in his own time lacked quality and attractiveness (Ferguson 1998, 2001). MacLeod was already well-known when he gained permission in the 1930s for the rebuilding of the ruined abbey of Iona as a place for training future Church of Scotland ministers who would serve in particular with the industrial poor. He promptly raised money, offered summer work to skilled craftsmen, and in what was in that era a major social departure offered young ministers and students as their untrained labour. Work started on the island marked by controversy and by the claim that he was creating an organisation 'half-way towards Rome, and half-way towards Moscow' (Ferguson 2001, 180). Nevertheless, in spite of breaks in wartime, the building was completed in the 1960s. It never fulfilled its original purpose but the abbey and other centres have since then received weekly paying guests. Members, however, as MacLeod intended, are dispersed and only spend a short time on the island during the process of joining the Community and during an annual gathering. Most live in Britain, and they meet regularly in local groups. They follow a rule which includes a strong commitment to action for social justice.

A fair amount has been written on the background to the Iona Community by two former Leaders (Ferguson 1998, Shanks 1999), while an oral history project was completed recently. In 2004 the BBC broadcast a radio play on the early days.

To most people the Community is associated with its centres on the island of Iona, at the site of the monastery founded by Saint Columba. Iona has been the focus of pilgrimage, tourism and a combination of both for centuries, and is today a place where people of differing lifestyles can meet and discuss social issues with a degree of freedom. The Community has had an impact in Scotland and beyond, partly because its charismatic founder developed some of the attributes of the 'Celtic' already linked to the island, to suit evangelical purposes, partly because of the popularity of its music and liturgy, and partly because of its Church of Scotland connections.

This touches one of the paradoxes in modern Celtic Christianity. The Community is expected by many to be a leading proponent, but it has an ambiguous relationship with the Celtic. It was founded by a male cleric with a military background and a strong social conscience, for men whose wives were not permitted to accompany them, and while the military sense has long gone, the concern for issues of social justice remains crucial. Still, a gentler aspect of the Community's early days is that it tapped into the earlier Celtic Revival and provided a link to the modern Celtic movement.

To do this, we need to look not only at its origins, but the history and situation of Iona, and the social situation on the mainland from which the Community grew and with which it interacted. This may also help us to understand something of the attractiveness of the Celtic, including the imagery it produced, the liturgies and music; and those aspects of organisation that have been emulated by other communities. It may also help to consider how the Celtic movement may have parted company with the energy that comes from pursuing social justice, and whether the two can be reconnected. We may look too at whether the Community has contributed through its island work to the strong sense of place in modern Celtic spirituality; how the Community is expected to be the custodian of ancient Celtic spirituality; and why this sits so uneasily with its understanding of itself. We might also consider in passing why the 'Celtic' has so little impact on the full-time residents of this Hebridean island itself.

Iona before the Community

When MacLeod and his followers came to Iona in 1938, they were not coming to an empty place but to an island with a crafting and fishing population, and ruins which have been sketched and interpreted by visitors for centuries. Historically, Iona had been a place of pilgrimage at least since it was settled by Saint Columba, in Irish Columcille, in the sixth century, and may have been a sacred place before then. Its Gaelic name, *Í*, probably means the 'island of yews'. The Columban monastery founded by Columcille survived until 1203, when a Benedictine monastery was built followed by an Augustinian nunnery. In the medieval period, Iona was part of the Norse kingdom and bishopric of Man and the Isles, but during the later Middle Ages English incursions onto the Isle of Man led to the diocese being divided and the abbey became the cathedral of the Isles. After the Reformation the monastic community died out, and the buildings, too large for the islanders' needs and too far from the centre of Scots power for alternative uses, slowly fell into disrepair (Brown and Clancy 1999, Power 2006).

There are accounts of the island dating from 1549, 1635, 1688, and about 1695. The buildings were apparently in a satisfactory condition when Dean Munro reported on the island in 1549 (Martin 1934, 498-500), but by 1635 the decayed condition of the church led King Charles I to order £400 to be sent for its repair (McNeill 1947, 49-50). The Hebridean Martin Martin found the domestic buildings in ruins in about 1698 and the abbey roof had also gone by the time Bishop Pococke visited in 1760 (Martin 1934, 286-91, Pococke 1887, 80, 83). The island may well have continued as a place of local pilgrimage, despite the restrictions of formal Presbyterian belief. A place where unbaptised children and murderers were buried is mentioned by Martin in 1698, and situated by Pococke, who only mentions the children, at the foot of one of the high crosses (Martin 1934, 287, Pococke 1887, 85).

As early as 1688 the visitor William Sachaverell exercised tourism combined with faith. Eighteenth-century visitors like Pococke, Thomas Pennant and others followed a similar pattern, and all did much the same as the writers in Chapter Three who interpreted ancient Scots and Welsh stories and texts to fit with their own literary and imaginative expectations of the Celtic. The visitors imposed their views on the island, in terms of how it had moved them and how it was likely to appeal to literary people of backgrounds similar to their own. Their writings speak of the decayed grandeur of the buildings and their effects on arousing the sentiments to prayer rather than upon the personal and individual experience which so attracts contemporary visitors. The best-known visitors included Samuel Johnson and James Boswell (1936, 330-39) during their tour of the Hebrides.

They were entertained as well as possible, given that there was 'not a drop of spirit upon the island', though the locals brewed a good deal of beer. Accommodation that night was basic, while mud, rubbish and cow-dung obscured some of the church floors, and the ruins on the whole caused disappointment.

Boswell returned alone after breakfast to say his prayers.

I then went into the cathedral, which is really grand enough when one thinks of its antiquity and of the remoteness of the place … I again addressed a few words to Saint Columbus … I read with an audible voice the fifth chapter of St James, and Dr Ogden's tenth sermon. I suppose there has not been a sermon preached in this church since the Reformation. I had a serious joy in hearing my voice, while it was filled with Ogden's admirable eloquence, resounding in the ancient cathedral of IcolmKill. (Boswell 1936, 334).

In fact, the islanders probably met in the ruined church for worship on Sundays, as Sachaverell had observed a century before.

Johnson comments:

But the fruitfulness of Iona is now its whole prosperity. The inhabitants are remarkably gross, and remarkably neglected: I know not if they are visited by any minister. The island, which was once the metropolis of learning and piety, has now no school for education, nor temple for worship; only two inhabitants that can speak English, and not one that can write or read. (Johnson 1819, 236.)

Sir Walter Scott might be expected to be a more sympathetic witness, but he recorded that the inhabitants were in a severe state of poverty and he was distressed by the condition of of the ruins. John Keats and the Wordsworths followed (Ferguson 1998, 43-5) and in 1828 the young Felix Mendelssohn was moved to high thoughts among the ruins and, like many visitors since, went on to Fingal's Cave on Staffa, a voyage marred by seasickness. Queen Victoria arrived by royal yacht, and sketched the ruins from it while her husband went ashore. Many others also visited and sketched both the abbey and the smaller but still substantial ruined nunnery.

Like the literary texts we have traced, the ruins were the background to religious expectations, social commentary and artistic interpretation that suited the time and culture of the visitor. Meanwhile, life for the locals went on much as in other parts of the Hebrides. While visitors enjoyed the ruins, the islanders were provided in the 1840s with a new Presbyterian Church and manse, on the eve of the Church of Scotland's Great Schism, which led to the rapid erection of a Free Church as well.

The next development was the rebuilding of the abbey church between the mid 1890s and the first decade of the twentieth century, at the instigation of the landowner, the then Duke of Argyll, in a period when other historical churches, such as Dunblane cathedral, were also rebuilt. At much the same time an Episcopalian retreat house was built on the island. In 1899 the landowner gifted the monastic sites to the care of Trustees on condition that they could be used for worship by all denominations. This was ahead of its time as it allowed not only services led by Episcopalians, Anglicans, like the Duke of Argyll himself; and by Presbyterians, the denomination of the island tenants; but also by others including, controversially, Catholics. Soon after the end of the First World War, it was suggested that the monastic buildings were rebuilt as well.

Another group of people had been present at the time of rebuilding of the church, and they also left their own interpretation of the island and its spirituality. From the 1870s onwards, in particular during the summer months, the island had a resident population of artists, mostly painters (Christian and Stiller 2000). They stayed at Iona's two hotels, sometimes leaving murals, or lodged with local people. While we do not know their views on the building work, the monastery and nunnery were sketched repeatedly from all angles. Unlike the earlier tourists who sketched only the ruins, some of these artists also depicted fishing and farming scenes. Most of the paintings, were, however, scenic, and especially popular were the sandy beaches at the island's north end. While some painters came to experiment in work on light, others came because the island was relatively accessible and was geared to being a holiday destination. Some hundred and fifty known artists visited between the 1870s and the later 1930s, but the high point was in the early years of the twentieth century when the Celtic Revival was in full swing. The island does not appear to have attracted many photographers and relatively few pictures of women and children have survived, though we know they were present and the island had its own school. Most of the insights we have are of how visitors, not inhabitants, understood Iona. By the 1930s the ferry company Caledonian MacBrayne, which ran the regular island services and also extra summer trips to the 'sacred isle', was commissioning scenic paintings for its advertising posters (Christian and Stiller 2000, 79-81).

The late-nineteenth-century painters were joined by writers, including William Sharp, who between 1894 and 1905 wrote twelve books as Fiona MacLeod. As well as his posthumously published *Iona* (1910) and his later poetry, there are books by him such as *The Sin-Eater and Other Tales* (1895) which contain a description that closely echoes the symbolist John Duncan's 1913 *St Bride*, a painting that shows her being taken in a dream to assist at the birth of Jesus. Sharp's widow Elizabeth selected five landscapes, three of Iona, by another leading Scottish artist, James Young Cameron, to illustrate her husband's collected works (Sharp 1910, Christian and Stiller 2000, 57-8). The folk-music collector Marjorie Kennedy-Fraser was a regular visitor on the island, while resident there were the silversmiths Alexander and Euphemia Ritchey. A significant library developed, containing mainly nineteenth-century works on history and Celtic Studies.

Although these visitors and the contemporary artists were to have a profound influence on the development of the 'Celtic' from their perspective of the Celtic Revival, the men who joined MacLeod, who were most of them previously unacquainted, lived alongside but apart from the island families and summer visitors to a military-style timetable that combined spirituality and hard work. From the start MacLeod produced a Community magazine *The Coracle* and used it to enlist support for the rebuilding programme on the island, for fundraising, for social activism on the mainland and as a forum for theological discussion. In 1941, it records that the day on Iona started at 6.45 am with 'reveille', followed by breakfast, worship, room inspection, worship, work, and hymn practice. The ministers received two daily 'lectures'. On this dry island, they got cocoa at 9.30 pm before lights out an hour later (*Coracle* 5 [1940], 14; 1941, 13). All those working on the rebuilding were expected to attend the two daily services, as photographs in the magazine pointedly attest, in working clothes. The Sunday programme was lighter but discipline remained strict. One account tells of how two of the men went to the uninhabited island of Staffa on a Sunday boat-trip, were marooned there but got a lift home with another boat, only to be 'gated' on Iona by MacLeod as a punishment. Wives were allowed to visit briefly, and many women were associates and fundraisers, but the Community membership remained exclusively male until 1969.

While support for the Community came from a wide range of people, many of the attitudes it held in its early days jar with a modern understanding of Celtic spirituality. Apart from the position of women, which was that of helpers, fundraisers, and staff, MacLeod, who accepted money from the rich, did not hesitate to refer to 'a humble soul in Glasgow, typical of many who encourage us' (*Coracle* 1941, 30-1). Equality might be the ideal in the rebuilding of the abbey, but in terms of intellectual output and social standing, MacLeod's Community was of its time.

He describes it in 1956 as having one hundred and forty members, thirty of them working abroad, and drawn from a variety of professions and occupations, although the large majority were young Church of Scotland ministers. There were hundreds of Associates and Friends, and a Community House in Glasgow provided opportunities for education, socialising and debate, in the centre of the city's deprived urban heartland (*Coracle*, 1956). It had been necessary too from an early date to accommodate on Iona people from varying backgrounds, many of whom were not regular churchgoers but who came to 'conferences' and later youth camps. These conferences dealt with such topics as 'Communism and Christianity', 'The Church and PsychoTherapy', and the abolition of the death penalty, but not 'Celtic' themes. Later, anti-nuclear activism developed too.

The rebuilding of the abbey on Iona was completed in the 1960s, by which time the Community had attracted people from well beyond Scotland, had developed youth work, and was influencing social action and regeneration in Scotland and beyond.

MacLeod and his colleagues continued work on their main concerns, the revival of Christianity, its expression in contemporary forms, and their commitment to social activism on behalf of the poor.

Worship remained as a key focus and on Iona was an essential part of the experience, one that was specifically presented as part of a monastic pattern, modelled on that of the Benedictine tradition of the medieval monastery. The Rule of Saint Benedict was interpreted as saying that work, study and prayer flowed into each other, and the aim was to express this ideal in a manner suited to family men of the Reformed Protestant traditions. `

There was also a strong emphasis, again developed from Benedictine practice, on good liturgy. An excellent speaker, MacLeod's own talks and religious services from Iona were broadcast from the 1930s onwards on the radio, which further increased their popularity. MacLeod and others produced the worship leaflets for use in the abbey, and attenders were requested not to remove them but to buy a copy at the abbey shop. As we have seen, they were not usually 'Celtic' in tone, and many of the liturgies would not meet modern ecumenical expectations, for they included prayers for the 'Universal and Early Church,' which named the Eastern Orthodox Church, the Reformed, Baptist, Methodist, Anglican and Lutheran Churches, the Society of Friends, and 'our own Communion [Church of Scotland]' (*Coracle* 1941, 17), but did not mention Catholics.

In other material written at this time by MacLeod, there are constant references to 'Celtic spirituality', though many of them must have been products of his own imagination and intended to fill the gaps in historical knowledge. They are frequently poetically moving in their expression, but they were there because the imagery, and the process of 'recovering' tradition, helped to make a point, and sometimes to deflect criticism.

An example is to be found in his treatment of the fourth century Saint Martin of Tours, 'one of the very greatest of our Celtic saints' (*Coracle* 1948, insert) . One of the ninth-century ring-headed crosses that stands outside the west door of the abbey is named after Martin, and the saint became a favourite of MacLeod's, and has since become a favourite of the current movement. According to one of MacLeod's friends, writing in *The Coracle*, Martin provided the copies of the scriptures that were brought by the early Christian Saint Ninian to Whithorn in Galloway, and which were ultimately copied by Saint Columba (Cattanach 1939, 13). The 1948 issue of *The Coracle* authoritatively declares that Martin had a Celtic father and Hungarian mother, while Ninian is said to have not only met him but to have studied at his abbey. The text, undoubtedly produced by MacLeod, goes on to matters more likely to be known in some way to their audience. Both Martin's abbey and the 'Celtic Church' are credited, as Presbyterians commonly believed, with being independent of Rome. Reference is made to the dating of Easter and the shape of the tonsure, issues taken from Bede's *Ecclesiastical History*. The account also makes the biblical Saint John the patron saint of the 'Celtic church', which is significant as another ring-headed but ruined cross on the abbey site is associated with his name. The reader is then referred to a photograph of the large, new, silver cross on the Abbey Communion Table, and informed that it represents in its Celtic ring-head style 'the sun of Creation superimposed upon a Cross' (*Coracle* 1948, insert). This is the crux of the argument, for the proposal of having a liturgical cross of any description, and on the replacement for a medieval altar, had aroused severe censure from within the Church of Scotland (Ferguson 2001, 194–5). MacLeod sought, by providing a 'Celtic' authority, to deflect in advance criticism from the General Assembly of the Church of Scotland and, perhaps even more, from the island's minister, with whom he was in serious disagreement.

MacLeod's interest lay in trying to create a common tradition for his own time, and he used the 'Celtic' as an extended image in order to connect with ancient ritual. With regard to a service of Holy Communion he writes:

> The form used is closely related to the early Celtic church and to the sequence of the Communion service of the reformers. But we do not follow it for that reason. We do it for the same reason as they did it – because by performing it in any age it makes available once more the experience of our membership together in Christ, and steels us to go sailing with him in the rescue of a shipwrecked world. (*The Abbey Services of the Iona Community* 1956, 16).

This introduction, however, is followed by a standard Church of Scotland service, although it also contains a few MacLeod intrusions, such as a 'Prayer of the Veil', and the following instruction concerning the elements for Communion:

These are to consist of loaves of bread from the Community House, Youth Centre and Fishing Station [now known as Camas], so that the whole life is brought forward. In the Celtic church, they so brought forward the 'ordinary bread' to be blessed and to be partaken of later at their midday meal.

Those directly associated with the Community were unlikely to have sufficient knowledge of the early 'Celtic Church' to be able to contradict MacLeod. The Celtic element was something that could be invoked in order to enable him to do what he felt was needed, but the actual practices have more in common with Eastern Orthodox tradition, and it is also this tradition that lies behind the 'Act of Belief', a service of personal commitment that occurred on Thursday nights.

Bread continues to be baked in the Community for Communion services, and another custom from this period also continues today. Small, specially baked biscuits were offered to the congregation on leaving the main church after the Sunday Communion, with the request to break and share them with a stranger in the cloisters, the area designated as the place of the 'common life'. This proved a highly effective means for enabling strangers to introduce themselves to each other. MacLeod claimed: 'This is Communion brought into the ordinary ways of life. This custom was practised in Iona in the sixth century' (*Abbey Services of the Iona Community* 1962?). There are no liturgical works surviving from the sixth century for Ireland and Britain, nor is this practice referred to in later texts, but it became identified as 'an ancient Celtic custom' and small oatcakes came into use. We need to look for origins not in the early church on Iona but in Greek and Russian Orthodox practice. The Greek practice of *antidoran*, involves bringing blessed bread to people not taking Communion at the end of the liturgy, a practice that could indeed have been followed in places during the sixth century. There is also the Russian practice of *prosphora*, of taking of blessed bread to people who were unable to attend church; and there is also the former tradition of '*pain sacré*', sacred bread', taken by those who did not receive Communion in the continental Catholic tradition. MacLeod may have invented the Celtic connection but his innovation worked on both the poetic and practical levels.

In general, MacLeod was most successful with practices like this and with aspects of liturgy that he introduced casually, in a context where there was neither the knowledge nor the courage to contradict him, and where his proposals met with approval. Already in the 1950s, Abbey Service Sheets were decorated with a picture of a Wild Goose, an image that remains on the Community's publishing imprint.

This 'Celtic symbol of the Holy Spirit' seems to have emerged from MacLeod's imagination in the late 1930s. Whether or not the deprived workers of Glasgow had ever seen a wild goose, or the local islanders had feasted on whichever breed he had in mind, the symbol became a potent feature of the Community's publicity (Ferguson 1988, Shanks 1999, 52-3). The design is based on the abstract interlace patterns of interweaving animals in the *Book of Kells*. MacLeod believed this had been produced on Iona, and once when the visiting Irish leader Éamon de Valera asked if he could help in any way, MacLeod jokingly asked if he would return it from Trinity College Dublin.

Images of shipwrecks, veils, and the Wild Goose (or at times Geese) are found repeatedly in MacLeod's poems, prayers, and polemical writings throughout his long life (*Coracle* 1 [1938], 3, MacLeod, 1985). When in his nineties, he completed a trenchant attack on what he saw as the spiritual devaluation of life by American policy and economic practice, with a 'Reverie' that draws together elements of many of his interests, and ends with reference to the later Irish prophecy attributed to Columba concerning the fall and revival of Iona:

> The Celtic symbol of the Holy Spirit is not a Dove. But the Wild Geese; flying high in V shaped formation, the leading bird from time to time giving way to another at the point of the V. True leadership is in Fellowship, taking the brunt by turn. Could the time come in the Abbey when Ecumenicity would be fully declared? One Sunday High Mass would be

celebrated. The next Sunday would be declared the primitive Presbyterian mode when the large common loaf would be shared round a long common table. We have recovered too the early Celtic Traditions that, as you leave the Church, you receive a piece of the Blessed Bread. This you then break with any stranger you have never met before – Communion out into all the world! And the next Sunday the Society of Friends would lead us in silent contemplation and then taking us to the Refectory to remember that every common meal is the Table of the Lord? Each in turn would take the brunt. The Holy Spirit would reveal Himself as fully as at the first free Pentecost. It has not happened yet. But Iona will be as it was.' (MacLeod 1972, 40)

Another common image that MacLeod was responsible for is that Iona is a 'thin place', a place where the 'veil is thin' (MacLeod, 1985, 60). The image comes from biblical texts concerning the veil of the Temple and the division between this world and the next, found in Saint Paul's Second Letter to the Corinthians and the Letter to the Hebrews 6:19. There are allusions to 'thin places' in Greek and Russian Orthodox tradition, which MacLeod also drew upon, such as the Greek Orthodox 'Feast of the Protecting Veil'. The biblical image can be seen too in the much-loved eighteenth-century hymn *Amazing Grace*, by John Newton (1725-1807). But in early twentieth-century literature the image is that the veil between the fairy world and the mundane world is thin. This may go back to the Scottish romantic writer George MacDonald and is used in this sense by Nicholas Stuart Gray in his popular 1962 novel for young people, *The Seventh Swan*. However, it is MacLeod's spiritual use of the 'thin place' imagery that has become firmly established, and is now also used about many other places which people sense have a particular spiritual quality. Even the usually sceptical liberal British newspaper *The Observer* quoted MacLeod describing Iona as 'a very thin place where only a tissue paper separates the material from the spiritual realm' (22 May 1994, 1) when it reported the burial on Iona of the British politician John Smith.

MacLeod provided the movement with good liturgy, a model of community and a base for people to meet each other. He also provided three keys images, the wild goose as the Holy Spirit; the ring-headed cross which unites the sun and the seasons; and the thin place, all of which have become defining symbols of Celtic spirituality. Among their many uses, the first gives the image of the pilgrim on the journey, while the last two can denote a place of arrival. These symbols are powerful, and provide the links between place and pilgrimage, freedom and stability, pre-Christian and Christian sacred space, wildness and continuity. Above all they provide an image of liminality, of moving at thresholds, of being on the edge. These have deep resonances because they touch aspects of faith not addressed in regular church life.

Like the belief that Celtic spirituality is holistic in a way church practice is not, these images have been adopted by other writers with the same intention of encouraging church renewal. Macleod explicitly wished to put poetry and romance into worship and spiritual reflection, and he may have been successful, if not in the ways he intended. We need now to turn from the impact of this powerful and poetic individual to another aspect of the Community's work, the development of its distinctive musical tradition.

The music

There was a choirmaster from the start of the Community's work on Iona, and music was always one of the attractions. There were already innovative developments in the 1950s and 1960s as a consequence of African influence, in particularly from Malawi and Zambia, transmitted through a Community member, Tom Colvin, who had been a missionary. However, the Community's Wild Goose Worship Group first became more widely known in the 1980s when it put new words to traditional Scottish and English folk tunes. According to the Community Member and hymn-writer John Bell:

> I think there were two books published by [Tom Colvin] which had his versions of African hymns with some rudimentary harmonisation, prior to folk tunes being used in the worship. It would be around the early 1980s – probably 1982/83 – that folk tunes began to be used.
>
> The reason was that Graham Maule and I were working for the Church of Scotland in Youth Work, and occasionally took people up to Iona. We realised from our mainland work

that young people were not singing in church and that was partly because the dominant hymnbook, published in 1973, was so obsolete.

We began (without any previous experience) to write hymns and set them to tunes which were common currency for us, as we both had parents who sang folk tunes in the house. We also believed that these were good vehicles to articulate the story songs about the life of Jesus, which were among our first contributions. These caught on and, particularly in the case of 'Will You Come and Follow Me?', 'A Touching Place' and 'We Cannot Measure How You Heal', they quickly established themselves in singing at the Abbey, partly because two of them were useful for services of healing and one for the service of commitment.

It was never our intention to put them into a wider circuit than the context in which they were first used ... among our voluntary staff in Glasgow and at particular services on the island.

I think there are two reasons which may contribute to their popularity. The first is that Calvinist Scotland was starved of any of its indigenous folk melody for almost four hundred years. The Psalms which were sung in the metrical version in the 16th century were set to tunes which had no ethnic origin in Scotland and compilers of successive editions of the *Church Hymnary* (published 1896) were happy to include English, Irish and Welsh folk tunes, but very reticent to deal with any material of a similar variety from Scotland.

So, for some people from this neck of the woods, being able to use their indigenous folk tunes was a bit of a novelty.

The second thing may have been that around the time ... there was a revival of interest in Celtic spirituality, and, for outside visitors, these songs were recognised as vehicles of that ethos.[1]

When the traditional Scottish and English folk tunes were published with new words in the 1980s, they added to what people were seeing as the 'Celtic' heritage, the more so because the Community was becoming more and more known for litur-

1. By e-mail to author 13/11/07.

gical experiment and hymnody, and this stretched beyond Scotland to England and the United States. The new hymns proved popular in England, perhaps because the generation taking a lead in church affairs would have known many of the tunes from their schooldays when the settings of traditional folk songs by Vaughan Williams and his contemporaries were widely used, and were sometimes also used for country dancing. Being familiar, they were fairly easily absorbed into church life, whatever surprises in terms of social justice the words might bring.

More recently, African and South American tunes have predominated in the music produced by Bell and Maule, with words in the indigenous languages as well as English. The words continue to place an emphasis on justice issues, but seem to be widely acceptable, a matter that brings into focus again one of the seeming contradictions of Celtic spirituality. People appreciate the music and enjoy what are seen as the Celtic resonances, but even though they may sing socially radical words, it does not mean that they will themselves become socially active.

The Community today

Iona today is a place of pilgrimage, similar in many ways to Lindisfarne and Bradwell-on-Sea, a place where people come, out of curiosity, or to explore their own spirituality, or because they are part of a church group developing its own sense of community, and perhaps enjoying a relatively inexpensive communal retreat or holiday. The islanders provide visitors' accommodation and there are also a number of other centres, including one owned by the unaffiliated spiritual Findhorn Community, the Episcopalian Church's Bishop's House, and a small Catholic retreat centre. Some people come for a spiritual experience or return regularly because they have had such an experience on the island. Others come because they believe that Iona has a particular immanent spiritual strength, and Druids and others may meet there. The island accommodates up to two thousand day-visitors in the summer months.

The centres owned by the Community are run by staff and volunteers, and are organised rather like the traditional holiday camps of a bygone era, with guests sharing accommodation with strangers and expected to participate in certain activities, including attending organised sessions and church services, and assisting with domestic tasks. The Christian ethos has to be accepted, but the volunteers may be present for a variety of reasons, including learning English. The Warden of the Abbey has traditionally been a member of the Community.

The Community now has some 280 members, who do not necessarily see the island as their focus. Joining this dispersed Community involves an interview and a two-year period of meeting and discernment, but allows the 'New Member' rather than the Community to decide whether to complete the process. Members renew their commitment annually, and in practice some leave, though the overall numbers continue to grow. The Community Rule includes daily prayer, including both the use of the Bible and prayer for other members; accounting to each other for the use of money and time; declaring one's income and parting with a tenth while also identifying how the remaining ninety per cent is used; meeting with each other regularly; and engaging in action for justice and peace. The best-known expression of this last commitment is non-violent protest against nuclear weapons outside the Faslane naval base in western Scotland, for which many have been arrested and some imprisoned. Other members are involved in various forms of activism in their own localities. In 2008 a commitment to environmental stewardship was added to the Rule.

Several members of the Iona Community have been prominent in the media and as public speakers beyond Scotland, including John Bell and Kathy Galloway, the former Leader, while one member, Ewan Aitken, is a senior figure in Edinburgh political life, and one, Margaret Legum (1933-2007), was a campaigning South African journalist. From a Community perspective, these are prominent people doing what less well-known members are also doing, in the fields of social justice rather than Celtic spirituality. None of this, however, prevents the Iona Community from being viewed from outside as the repository for an ancient and recoverable Celtic tradition.

While many members of the Community publish regularly, including for *The Coracle* and for the Community's Wild Goose imprint, very few write on Celtic spirituality or history. It is the liturgies and in particular the music of the Wild Goose Worship

Group, together with the understanding of Iona as a distant place to visit in the Hebrides, that give people the expectation that the Community and its island centres are the home of Celtic spirituality. Other less established centres have made much more of their Celtic roots, but Iona remains the focus of all things Celtic to many of its visitors from across the world. As a consequence, the island staff often provide something 'Celtic' to meet these expectations.

Most of the Community would not identify with the 'Celtic' except in a general way. More tellingly, and perhaps relevant to the general belief that Celtic Christianity was spontaneous and lightly structured, some of the members and prospective members may struggle to identify with the traditional expectation of being involved in their local church. It may be for some, like many visitors, they might find within the Community and its centres the opportunities to discuss issues of faith that are not normally addressed within formal church structures. Even for the members who work for the churches, including as ministers, it may be that these opportunities are significant, and the Community provides fellow-travellers and a place of safe transition. While the Community requires a relatively high level of personal commitment and shared values, including a commitment to Christian witness, it requires the individual member to identify how these commitments are being fulfilled, and indeed, how deep the commitment is. If an increasing number of members, applicants and associates perceive themselves as on the fringes of church life and are looking for alternative ways of relating to others in a faith context, this may show us something of how church life is changing. Iona and its centres may attract those who regard themselves as post-church, with limited or no current church connection, as much as those in search of Celtic spirituality.

Other Communities
Dispersed religious communities are not all Celtic, but there are some that are similar to the Iona Community in their organisation, ecumenical commitment and the ability to attract members who feel on the edge of institutional churches. Most of these communities are concerned with spirituality more than social

action, and are more consciously 'Celtic'. It is worth looking for comparison at one organisation that was founded by a contemporary of MacLeod but which is not driven by Celtic agenda, and then to consider more the recent communities that are.

Othona

The Othona Community at Bradwell-on-Sea in Essex was established in 1946 by an Anglican clergyman and Royal Air Force chaplain, Norman Motley, an acquaintance of MacLeod. Under his leadership, groups had been praying together during the Second World War, and his vision was to enable them and Londoners to meet together afterwards, and also to attempt reconciliation with Germans. Motley acquired land on the coast at Bradwell-on-Sea in Essex, not far from London, beside a Saxon chapel. This battered sixth-century building is made of stones salvaged from an abandoned late Roman coastal fort mentioned by Bede and from which the Community takes its name. The chapel is still in use and is the focus of an annual pilgrimage organised by the Anglican Diocese of Chelmsford, but it is also encountered unexpectedly by walkers of the coastal path. It was built by the Northumbrian bishop Cedd, and can therefore be regarded as part of the original 'Celtic church', though for Motley, unlike MacLeod, the vision came first and the ancient building seemed the appropriate focus. Motley ran Othona in the post-war period as a spiritual holiday home for Londoners, with an approach derived from a combination of his military background with secular models such as Butlin's holiday camps, and like Iona as a way to enrich appreciation of the Christian faith.

A second centre was later acquired in Dorset, and like Iona, both centres continue to run themed retreats and weekend events, as do many retreat houses, but Othona also has the shared accommodation that most have abandoned. The Othona Community continues to provide for Londoners, and is also used by school groups. Like Iona, where there was once an attempt to heat the Abbey by electricity generated from the sea, the Bradwell-on-Sea site was an early experimenter with energy efficiency and waste disposal, and retains an environmental agenda. Othona too has a dispersed Community, though day-to-day organisation is in the hands of a core of active members. Its rule is explicit in the need not only to pray and work but also to study and to play together.

The Othona Community in Essex feels remote, and is approached by relatively minor roads, though it is in reality not far from London. The coastal path is used by walkers who also encounter a wildlife sanctuary and a large power station nearby. While the annual pilgrimage is attended by thousands of churchgoers, Othona is a relatively little-known centre and there is little of the sense of arrival dear to city dwellers who venture to Iona.

The Othona Community developed at much the same time as the Iona Community, to fill different needs, and the two leaders' personal acquaintance did not lead to a lasting connection. It remains an interesting parallel, a centre that is not specifically Celtic but which, because of its Anglo-Saxon chapel in Essex, has the Celtic attributed to it.

Corrymeela

The Corrymeela Community similarly did not start out to be 'Celtic' but has been influenced by it.

It was established in Northern Ireland in 1965 by a Presbyterian minister Ray Davey and his associates. It was initially a Protestant organisation, though it later admitted Catholics to full membership. Students from Queen's University of Belfast, where Davey was chaplain, predominated in its early years. It moved far from this background in response to the changing political and social nature of Northern Ireland, and its role is currently changing again in the light of the political settlement and also the diminishing funding for reconciliation work. Although little known in the early days of the Troubles, its significance grew over the years and it has had a role in Northern Ireland's recent social history through its provision of a 'safe space', especially for those from impoverished backgrounds in the areas most prone to violence. It enabled people to get away, meet those from 'the other side', and in some cases talk at a deep level. There was some quiet engagement with political or paramilitary groups during the Troubles, and some of its members, particularly clergymen, were involved for short periods at a high level. Many lesser-known figures had considerable impact in ensuring that communications between rival political entities were kept open. Funded rather than supported by bodies with an interest in the cessation of the Troubles, it is often referred to publicly as a key player in reconciliation work.

While situated on a wild and beautiful coast that can itself provide a sense of liminality, Corrymeela's buildings do not have the ancient sense of place of Iona, an island which has been inhabited since pre-historic times. Its venue was on the market in the early 1960s and appeared suitable.

While Celtic events are part of the Corrymeela programme and liturgy, the Community has not intentionally taken on a Celtic agenda, and the recently-published history of the Community by the former journalist Alf McCreary uses the word 'Celtic' only twice (McCreary 2007). Corrymeela's printed liturgical resources utilise other material, especially from Iona, but the Community does not generally 'celticise' the material it receives. The 'Celtic' has been little used and then in a low-key manner as a potential tool for reconciliation. In view of the fact that traditionally both Protestants and Catholics have claimed to be the true inheritors of the early Irish church, this was presumably a conscious decision to prevent the Celtic from becoming a source of division rather than healing. Further, there were claims during the 1980s from Protestants as well as Catholics that it was they who were descended from the original inhabitants of north-east Ireland, with the implication that they had the main right to be there. While the Corrymeela Community avoided these sources of division, it shows that the general understanding of the 'Celtic' as something shared across all the Christian churches could still become a source of division if its use appeared to promote one tradition over another.

The Corrymeela Community was influenced by the Iona Community in terms of its organisation, and with some 140 members it functions not unlike the Iona Community, with small local groups meeting regularly, and a strong emphasis on working for peace. It is a predominantly Protestant community, and like the Iona Community, largely middle-class though, unlike the Iona Community, it now has only a handful of clerics among its members. An early Leader, John Morrow, was a member of the Iona Community and some members, including his son Duncan Morrow, who currently leads the Community Relations Council, and Brendan McAllister, who is a Victims Commissioner, have achieved prominence in Northern Ireland. Since the cessation of the Troubles, the prayer house belonging to the Community and other centres, including one based at Armagh cathedral, have become much more open to the use of the 'Celtic' as a tool for ecumenical spirituality.

The Community of Aidan and Hilda

We have already considered the role of the Northumbria Community in the development of the Celtic. Another Northumbrian Christian group, The Community of Aidan and Hilda, is based on Holy Island, Lindisfarne. There are no visible remains of the monastery founded from Iona in the late sixth century, but the ruins of the medieval re-foundation attract many visitors. The island is regarded by many as the centre of the English 'Celtic Church', and the Community has the benefit of the sense of place this confers.

Joining, becoming a 'Voyager', of the Community of Aidan and Hilda includes having an *anamchara*, a soul-friend, and going through a discernment process not unlike that required by the Iona Community. Again, the Community is dispersed but has a mother-house which receives guests. Resident is the Guardian, one of the Founders, Ray Simpson, a prolific writer on Celtic spirituality, who comes from a high Anglican rather than an evangelical tradition. His approach has been compared to that of a romantic novelist for his creativity in developing new concepts of the Celtic. Simpson has taken his subject and the Community ethos to other European countries.

The centrality of Lindisfarne for the English form of Celtic Christianity was reinforced by the writings of David Adam, who was for many years the vicar. A number of other small groups also offer hospitality and prayer on this tidal island.

Other expressions

A small community emulating the Iona Community formed for a time among the many expressions of spirituality at Glaston-bury in Somerset, the home also of a very small Celtic Orthodox Church which regarded itself as benefiting from roots that go back to the centuries before the Great Schism (Bowman 2004, 276). Other communities have grown from time to time, but do not seem to have been a direct response to new understanding of the 'Celtic' as much as attempts to find new ways to express Christianity in community.

Celtic Christianity has had an impact further afield. It has become popular in Germany, and increasingly also in Sweden. Norway has a potential equivalent to Iona in the ruins of the medieval monastic buildings on the island Seljø, south-west of Trondheim, which are associated with the mythical Irish saint, Sunniva. The Community of Aidan and Hilda also functions in Norway. There is increasing interest in all things Celtic in Greece, and in a twist to MacLeod's fascination with the Orthodox tradition, one of Peter Tremayne's Sister Fidelma novels which is set at the Synod of Whitby has been translated into Greek (Tremayne 1994; Bowman 2004, 276).

Conclusions

The Iona Community did not set out to identify itself as specifically 'Celtic', but when an interest developed in the 1980s it found that others expected it to be at the heart of the Celtic movement. Given Iona's significance in the Celtic Revival of later nineteenth-century Scotland and the publicity gained during the rebuilding of the abbey, this was probably inevitable. The 'Celtic' element owes its origins to the work and reputation of one forceful and poetic writer, George MacLeod, who used images from published sources and from his own imagination to serve the perceived needs of his time and church. Knowing that his experiments in worship and his social activism made him a controversial figure, he produced 'Celtic' roots to countermand criticism. His approach relied on the Presbyterian view of religion found in Scotland and Northern Ireland, that the Reformed tradition was the purest form of the Early Church. Consequently, what could be 'reclaimed' or 're-discovered' could be presented as part of the Reformed heritage. The absence of references to Catholicism may be due in part to a desire to ensure that the liturgical practices based on Orthodox Christianity were not misinterpreted as Catholic. However, he would also have been aware of the view among the Glasgow Irish that they were the true, direct successors of the universal Early Church and of its 'Celtic' version.

The term 'Celtic' was used in this period largely as an extended metaphor. For MacLeod it provided an imaginative dimension to the Community's work, and as no one he worked with had the specific knowledge or the will to challenge him, his interpretations became established as fact. Macleod and others saw the 'Celtic' as a tool for mission and for good-quality liturgy. When new 'Celtic' concepts developed in the later twentieth century, there was an expectation that the island, and the Community, would be in the forefront of the Celtic movement, not least because of the music that used native folk-tunes and the liturgies that used prayers based on the *Carmina Gadelica*. However, most members saw their priorities elsewhere.

CHAPTER SEVEN

Reclaiming the Sealskin, Restoring the Woven Cord and Chasing the Wild Goose: A medley of metaphors and a question of use

We have considered the historical background to the early Christian churches in these islands; the ways in which the concept of an ancient Celtic church were formed by previous generations, especially through the use of printed texts; the selection of works regarded as relevant in the later twentieth-century for mission and spiritual development; the themes that emerged and the ways in which a body of literature was extracted, pruned, accepted and then transmitted again; and the way in which the influence of the powerful founder of a Christian Community, combined with innovations in music and liturgy, fed into the movement's expectations of the Celtic. We now turn briefly to some of the uses, and then to some of the theological questions raised by modern Celtic spirituality.

There are some obvious ambiguities: the concept of the 'Celtic' includes England; the movement portrays the early Celtic world as full of variety and spontaneity but treats it as a unity; it extols the natural world and the inter-connectedness of all the created order but has little social agenda other than general environmental concerns; it has a post-modern community of networks and para-church organisations but its Christianity remains orthodox; many of its products were intended as tools for mission but appeal to people at the edges of established church life; it emphasises a connectedness with ancient traditions yet responds to contemporary social expectations on equality and the place of women. It holds a tension between the safe and the wild – the excitement of the divine as perceived through a Celtic prism. It is relatively little grounded in the reality of early Christianity in these islands, or the later folk cultures of the fringes, yet it speaks to people today. Tentative suggestions on some of these aspects have already been offered, and this chapter seeks to draw together some of the threads, approaching the subject from several directions, and asking questions rather than trying to reach conclusions.

From the perspective of this writer, Celtic Christianity undoubtedly works. It is a movement owned by the indigenous populations of Britain and Ireland, and it is noticeable that it has almost no adherents from the newer ethnic minorities. It functions in an otherwise declining church society that is fed by groups which provide musical, liturgical and devotional material which people find supportive and spiritually enriching. It also provides models for the formation of communities, some of which have survived for decades. These sustain and support people who are looking beyond the current models of church, have found them damaging, or who simply do not have contact with them.

At the same time, much of the content has been taken up by mainstream churches, a process which allows the movement to be owned by them, and made respectable. Books on the subject, commentaries and other input are regular fare in the church media, and the contemporary understandings of the movement are rarely questioned.

There are parallel developments in church life at the start of the twenty-first century. Both the Church of England and the Methodist Church have recently given attention, and funding, to 'new ways of being church', through experimenting with the time, place and structure of religious activities. There is an emphasis on providing new forms of spirituality for people to chance upon while engaging with other activities. Termed 'Fresh Expressions', these can include 'Café Church', informal worship over a cup of coffee; 'messy church'; 'liquid church' or other ways of connecting with people who might have little or no formal Christian practice, ideally through the kind of networking or activity already familiar to them, and in places they frequent. The intention is that these activities will lead to a deeper understanding and commitment. These forms of experimentation are encouraged by the church hierarchies, although there are criticisms from within their bodies that this is 'religion-lite', a dumbing-down of essential beliefs or a catering for people's expectations of choice rather than commitment and inner growth. Another criticism is that, as many of them are dependant on the inspiration of a leader, usually a full-time paid leader, they are unlikely to survive a change in staff or an end to funding. In areas of deprivation they may be one of a succession of 'options' made available by outsiders to a regeneration-weary resident population, but in more affluent areas they may be regarded as pleasant alternatives to other drop-in, drop-out activities. Whether they lead people to more regular commitment of faith, time and money, and whether they have any lasting impact, it is too early to say, but the mainstream churches are putting effort into these kinds of activities in the hope of engagement with people who do not normally involve themselves with church life.

One role of the 'Celtic', especially through resources from communities like Iona, may be that they provide a form of 'Fresh Expressions' for people already active within Christianity who are looking for new ways of experiencing it. However, there may be the same questions on whether they go on to develop their spirituality and commitment, from a level they have chosen to a stage, essential to all religious communities, where they put aside autonomy in order to benefit the group, in doing so growing in personal faith.

For this, we return to the question of liminality and to those people at a turning point in church life. The movement provides a sense of wildness and excitement in the quest for the divine, but its adherents are mainly people from the most stable sector of society. One of the attractions may be that it provides a safe means of spiritual rebellion against institutional Christianity. This may at some level be recognised, and just as adolescents are given certain freedoms in order to retain them within church life, questioning adults can, through using the insights of modern Celtic spirituality, be accommodated by the institutions, while being able to experiment intellectually and spiritually.

The 'Celtic' may at times also act as a panacea to tired, over-stressed church-people. The movement and what it has given means much to some people, but it is also possible to embrace the Celtic without working hard. As well as books, there is music, and the pentatonic scales and the rhythmic cadences emulating the *Carmina Gadelica* can be suited to gentle meditation. The hymns from the Iona Community are indeed challenging but like the liturgies seem to be used by congregations that do not feel challenged. Singing about social justice may not translate directly to a lifestyle that engages with the poor in society or with cutting-edge campaigning. While going to the edge is the ideal, the actual physical travel to places like Iona and Lindisfarne is less demanding than many holidays abroad. It is possible to go metaphorically to the edge while having a safety net.

But this is only part of the movement. Because it has become rooted in contemporary needs, we need to explore whether it can be rooted enough to be of use.

Can the historically wrong be theologically right?
Theology is the exploration of the nature of God, and contemporary theology concerns the perception of the relationship between God and creation at this particular time. If Celtic spirituality is regarded as a path to God, we need to consider why this movement has developed in the later twentieth century and what purpose it is serving.

We have seen that much of what passes for Celtic Christianity bears no relation to the times or places in which the poetry and prose we enjoy were created. Whether these were Celtic or Anglo-Saxon, they are used out of context, sometimes in forms that have deviated very far from the originals, and sometimes in forms that have been silently pruned. The Last Celtic Twilight used the translations of poetry and prose such as saints' lives that became available as the contemporary academic study of Celtic developed, and some poets and more artists took the themes and the styles of translation and developed their own works. The contemporary movement uses the same texts but has placed a much greater emphasis on the production of new poetry and prayers, which have in turn become part of the modern canon. Yet, with all these limitations, Celtic Christianity speaks to a large number of people who take it as real and suited to the western world today. It seems to touch aspects of people's spiritual lives that are not being fed by the churches.

Christian theology presupposes that God can work through unintentional ignorance, as well as through knowledge. So we need to consider whether the evidence, the 'fruits of the Spirit' seem to be working through the current Celtic movement and those who come into contact with it. If this is the case, from a Christian perspective, Celtic spirituality is a means by which they relate to God. Celtic spirituality has been criticised for its limited use of sources, for being naïve, but not for being destructive. It does not mean that the relationship is sufficiently strong to be a life-long resource rather than a stepping stone.

Christian theology and practice since at least the time of Saint Benedict have emphasised the need for study, for access to original texts, for time to contemplate them, to relate them to the scriptures and to the reflective thinking of others upon them. Most contemporary books rely on selections by people who have not studied the sources. A question arises when writers extol the subject, finding new takes and new relevancies for today's society, but rely on their contemporaries' views rather than pursuing study through courses on Celtic Studies and learning one of the relevant languages. We would expect those who write on the scriptures to study of the texts. Even its most enthusiastic adherents regard Celtic spirituality as supplementary to the scriptures, but it can be questioned whether the lack of sufficient original material is limiting the capacity of Celtic spirituality to help readers grow. This is not to suggest that everyone will have the time and inclination for such study, but only that books intended to influence others may need more depth.

One of the reasons may be a fear that a more intellectual approach will cramp the style and enthusiasm of the writers and speakers. Yet, many of the scholars who spent months and years on the fine detail of editing ancient texts in obscure languages, were also poets in love with their subject. The pursuit of knowledge does not necessarily lead to spiritual dryness, and the labour put into understanding the original usually shows in the finished product. An academic pursuit of the texts does not prevent them from being relished artistically or spiritually, but is more likely to increase the pleasure.

What the modern practitioners have done may be viewed as paralleling on a smaller scale the construction of the scriptures. The Old Testament in particular is regarded by most Christians as a series of books written over a long period of time, containing the Word of God as it has been transmitted through people over the centuries. Most modern 'Celtic' practitioners have not treated their work as carrying similar weight, but it can be argued that some knowledge of the original texts in their original contexts will enrich the spirituality both of the practitioners and those whom they seek to influence, just as it has done for the study of the scriptures.

The lack of connection to original sources poses a problem for a movement that is fundamentally English Protestant in its origins. The leaders of the Reformation were adamant that people should have direct access to the scriptures, so they could read the Word of God, although in translation, and judge for themselves. This was considered worth dying for. Yet many writers of the movement, while espousing this approach to scripture, are in effect cutting their readers off from knowledge of the richness of Celtic religious prose and poetry. This is happening at a time when modern technology is making access to the printed word ever easier. There is certainly a role for modern authors in selecting material and making suggestions on usage, but leaving references and other markers to the originals is respectful to their readers and a benefit for future generations.

The practitioners may argue that there are parallels to their methods in the current usage of scripture. Common church practice is that selected short sections are used in liturgy, and a context is provided if at all by the preacher or through group reflection. While this is an accepted approach, the methods of selection mean that some passages are rarely used and others are silently cut. Among many other instances of pruning, the Catholic Office of Morning and Evening Prayer uses Psalm 63 while seeing no need to point out that it has cut the final, violent, verse, and those aware of this have not deemed this treatment unacceptable. However, it is also true that a reader of Psalm 63 is more likely to know where to find the unexpurgated text than is the reader of a contemporary anthology of Celtic spirituality.

How scholars respond also needs theological consideration. In order to redress the tendency to cut and select without reference to context, some academics have tried to find a way to integrate the study of early Christianity in these islands into modern Celtic spirituality. Sometimes they may seem to stretch the evidence in their desire to encompass and direct the movement, perhaps because the balance between their core beliefs and their expertise is in question. Certainly, current scholars such as those edited by Atherton (2002), and also Allchin and de Waal (1986) and Davies and Bowie (1995) might at times be regarded as reading in evidence, or giving personal rather than scholarly opinion. This can be a problem when writing for more than one audience, for those with a scholarly knowledge may make distinctions not always clear to interested lay readers.

A personal view is that the attempts to steer the movement have not to date been particularly influential, but the desire to do so by increasing the quality and range of the texts, to present them to a wider audience, is essential if the movement is to develop. To take another angle, Janet Backhouse's work on the Lindisfarne Gospels and Carol Farr's on the iconography of the *Book of Kells* indicate how study of these works shows us how to understand and appreciate what may be attractive, but at first sight has little to offer in terms of spirituality. Backhouse, Farr and others demonstrate the theological content, the extent of international influences, and the levels of cultural sophistication of the original artists and their audiences in the early churches in these islands. These insights assist a modern audience to appreciate both the aesthetic and the spiritual value of what has survived, which is probably only a fraction of what was originally produced. Those who work with the texts may be uncovering similar veins of native wealth.

On the other hand, the texts are works of art, intended for an audience, and as such will speak to people in different ways that may be respectful to the original. We interpret art for our own generation, its expectations and its needs. The role of the scholar is to provide the best possible interpretation, and it then passes into the hands of a wider audience.

It seems that Christian spirituality needs the backbone of academic knowledge to keep it balanced. This allows experimental interpretations to enrich it, but also provides points of reference to validate them, using both the body of acquired knowledge and the experience of the praying community. The works selected or produced by the current Celtic movement that will most probably survive are those which relate best to the body of traditional knowledge.

Modern Celtic spirituality is already a generation old and a process of sifting seems to have happened already. Although the movement is very dependant on the printed word, the sifting is similar to a process that takes place in oral tradition, and also in folk music. This process usually enables the more substantial material to be retained, while the more light-weight vanishes. While the intensely personal does not usually last, the variations of a good performer can extend the traditional repertoire and keep it alive and open to contemporary needs. On the other hand, in the storytelling tradition, poor interpretations are more likely to survive at times of decline and dissolution in language and loss of traditional culture. If something similar happens where popular theology and spirituality are concerned, the Celtic movement may need to draw upon the work of sympathetic scholars, to ensure the movement remains broad enough to keep its connection with the universal church heritage. It may be that the Celtic has a particular role to play at a time when in Ireland the traditional expectations of church appear to be collapsing, while in Britain church practice has been in a long, slow decline.

This chapter began with the titles of three books. Annie Heppenstall-West's activity book with pull-outs (2004) refers to a popular folk-tale that was perhaps influenced by the interpretation of Helen Julian (2004, 77-8) who sees singing to seals as acting in a Celtic tradition that provides a personal sense of continuity with the past. The second work is intended to aid church renewal, and the author tells us that while restoring the woven cord of the title is technically impossible, he prefers to think more poetically than scientifically (Mitton 1995, 9). The third title (Ferguson 1998) carries an image of evocative power, the wild goose. The titles resonate with elements of the current movement where the theological content may seem slender.

Let us now look at the intentions of the authors and the spirituality of the audience.

Building on foundations: the fruits of study and the fruits of beauty
As we have seen, the writings that make up the canon of contemporary Celtic Christianity were greatly influenced by the last Celtic Twilight. This literary and aesthetic movement, like

other similar movements in Europe, fed a sense of national pride and identity. A country's own literary heritage could be presented as brought back from the brink of oblivion, equal in range and quality to that of any other country. In Ireland and Scotland, these considerations gave us the literature that has made the current, spiritual, movement possible.

The nineteenth- and twentieth-century writers responsible for the published works we have used were thoroughly familiar with Christianity, and several of them are known to have had a personal belief. Promoting their religious convictions may not have been their intention, but when we look at what they selected and published it becomes clear that this was important to them. In turn, their selection was what became known to the people who 'rediscovered' the Celtic. This was especially true in England, where there was less knowledge of the ongoing publication of the texts and translations from the Celtic languages, and perhaps even less of the remaining folk tradition.

Apart from a personal faith, another factor is the beauty the earlier writers found. Those who collected folk tradition and those who selected from written works in defunct languages, did so because they found beauty, a high artistic quality in their texts. They believed that they could be lost, and wanted to share them with a wider readership. Most academics have gone into their work through the love of their subject, and when their subject is aesthetically pleasing, they are likely to select what moves them and may move others too. Fortunately, Alexander Carmichael, Kuno Meyer, Eleanor Hull and James Carney were also poets and could present their material in a way that appeals powerfully today, while Greene and O'Connor worked collaboratively to do the same. We need therefore to consider the fact that they loved their subject and were willing to labour to produce the best possible versions so that others could enjoy them too. They may also have wished that some readers would explore the originals and make more of them accessible too.

This leads us to consider whether love for the subject can itself provide a connection with the spirituality of the original writers. The material was 'recovered' by scholars through love, labour, sometimes personal faith, and a desire to do right by the authors, who would presumably have welcomed a wider audience. We may consider whether, from a faith perspective, works produced to these ends are 'fruits of the Spirit' and pathways to the divine.

This relates to the theology of beauty, the capacity of beauty, as an expression of the divine, to itself become a pathway to God which transcends time and place. There is a theological tradition of love as a force of transmission and a unifying force, of reading through charity, with Christ illuminating the process. Even when the intention of producing and transmitting a text or work of art is not specifically devotional, this Augustinian approach to theology suggests that love can be transmitted through the common appreciation of beauty.

The early twentieth-century scholars had their limitations in how they handled material, and we may see them as too romantic in their approach; too full of nationalist fervour and desire to promote their native culture as equal to more dominant cultures; and too ready to accept a continuity between ancient and folk poetry. However, they were scholars of skill and integrity, working as their subject developed, and they could not have forseen how their material would be re-used in later contexts. We need to consider whether a similar integrity, a similar respect for the beauty, including the strangeness as well the familiarity of beauty, the seeing the known from a new perspective, was applied to their sources by more recent writers.

From the artistic point of view, there are poets who do not know the original languages and their contexts but can still produce sensitive modern poetry for devotional use, as did Kate McIllhagga (2004), on the basis that this is all that is intended. This also needs to be considered from the perspective of transmitting beauty, of connecting with the known and with the new insights a work of art has given.

There are also a number of recent scholars who, like their predecessors, have made significant, and sometimes artistic, contributions. Because the spiritual movement has grown in the intervening years, there can be difficulties when the scholar writes from within Celtic spirituality. An example is Mary Low whose *Celtic Christianity and Nature* (1996) suffers from a lack of clarity about what is original and what is her personal interpretation. However, Low's declaration that the early Celtic Christians had an overwhelming sense of the beauty of the world (1996, 38-9), a view shared by Bradley (1993, 32, 39), is hard to refute, and allows us to look at one very significant contribution made by Celtic spirituality to modern theology.

Modern readers respond to the material that writers like Low present, to the way it mixes the strange and the familiar, to the imagery drawn from the natural world. The poems and prose feed into our current concerns about the environment and stewardship for succeeding generations. They move us because they are beautiful and help the reader to appreciate the natural world. Theologically, if they raise conscience about how we treat the world and our neighbour, they are presumably a tool of the divine, even if their current usage would have been incomprehensible to the original composers. If within Christian circles the 'Celtic' has become a metaphor for holistic and environmentally sensitive behaviour, which assists people to make the connections between individuals' actions and the health of the planet, this must be a valid path for contemporary Christians even if it had no historical part in the shaping of the source material. A reading through a theology of charity, where the beauty is what makes it transmissible, has practical outcomes for the well-being of others.

This brings us to another consequence of the artistic beauty of our sources. It has been said that the Celts used imagery rather than theological language. This may be overstating the case because formal theology was usually expressed in Latin, but it is true that the Gaelic languages do not have much theological vocabulary, and imagery plays a vital part in folk prayer, as it also does in love songs and other aspects of life. Many of the stories of the saints selected by recent writers are about those who meet God in closeness to nature. The selectors regard this closeness as a reason to conserve the natural world because it is a place where God is present. Therefore, nature poetry expressed in the first person, and the telling of stories about people regarded as close to God, are important means of conveying essential truths. The emphasis is on alluding rather than instructing, portraying aspects of Christian doctrine from a fresh angle. These are aspects of what is known as narrative theology.

Telling the story

A love of the natural world and the enduring human need for stories may help to explain the 'rediscovery' of the saints, including the saints from England. Stories with some depth and much quirkiness are used to supplement biblical ones, and may be regarded as more freely adaptable to suit personal or contemporary interpretations. They may also satisfy a need for heroes. They are stories for adults, and they may be filling a hunger.

A trend in late twentieth-century theology has been rediscovering the importance of narrative, of storytelling. This can be at the level of the main, overarching story, the meta-narrative, which is in Christian terms the life, death and resurrection of Jesus, and the invitation to people through the ages to partake in this story. There is also the level of smaller stories that portray some aspect of the overarching narrative that is found in the New Testament and in church history. This approach is sometimes described as post-liberal or post-modernist, and represents a turn from theological approaches that emphasised the individual and engagement through conversation. The use of narrative and allusion can sit well with the earlier stages of mystical engagement, especially through the natural world.

Narrative theology has a specific use in Christianity as Jesus of Nazareth was a consummate storyteller who clearly gave unexpected twists to known stories. We can also assume by comparison that, in a largely illiterate culture, his audience had a sophisticated response to story. While we do not have this immediate response today, narrative approaches attempt to present in story form significant truths for adult listeners, to reclaim what has more or less been relegated to the world of early childhood or to the television drama as a serious and enjoyable means of communication.

Church services extract small pieces of scripture and use them as a basis for communal prayer and sermons. Often a narrative relating to Jesus or one of his parables is used. A modern audience is used to sound-bites and finds this length familiar, and most church-goers are generally familiar with the overall context. Many of the stories from the saints' lives which are used today are similarly extracted from longer accounts. Sources included the 'Religion' section of Kenneth Jackson's *A Celtic*

Miscellany and Helen Waddell's *Beast and Saints*. Bede's works are particularly popular in an English context, for he was a master storyteller, but pieces of similar length are also extracted from Irish, Scottish and Welsh sources, often through a popular edition of the life of an individual saint. The use of relatively small extracts seems to work well, and the stories are seen as in some way relevant to the reader and current concerns. There have also been some attempts to re-write them.

One of the uses of Celtic spirituality is then the desire to recover storytelling. While stories occur throughout western Christian tradition, the practice is regarded as Celtic. It concentrates almost exclusively on narratives about the saints, and relatively little used is one different, and outstanding, piece of narrative theology from the seventh-century, the Old English *Dream of the Rood*, to which we shall turn in the next chapter.

It remains doubtful whether recounting stories, or creating new ones, can alone be sufficient for developing the more mature spirituality that many of its adherents are seeking. This brings us to the next subject.

Can the derivative aid spiritual development?
In this book we have considered Celtic spirituality as a phenomenon that reflects contemporary concerns. To understand how, if at all, it is seen as enabling a quest for the divine, we need to look further at why so many people are using it. For this we can turn to one particular model of Christian spiritual development.

The American writer James Fowler, in his book *Stages of Faith* (1995) suggested that there are six stages in the life of faith, stages through which both individuals and churches can pass. His theory was taken up by Alan Jamieson in *A Churchless Faith* (2002), and others have used it in various contexts to help understand why traditional churches are decreasingly attracting people but interest in spirituality appears to be flourishing. Both Fowler and Jamieson claim that not all stages are experienced by everyone, that many people 'equilibrate' at a certain stage, that all stages are equally morally valid and that each can provide spiritual satisfaction. However, there is a natural progression between them.

Fowler's original work remains important to our under-

standing but Jamieson's more recent insights and language are
especially relevant. To summarise Jamieson's argument, a life of
faith starts in the stage of innocence and acceptance, natural to a
young child. It then passes naturally to a literalist stage where
experiences are organised and categorised. This stage develops
at the age of about six in western culture, but for some people it
is where they remain for life. The next stage, at which most
church members remain, is the loyalist stage at which the community and conformism are highly significant, and God is understood mainly as external and transcendent. The natural progression is through a difficult transition, which can last for
years, into a fourth, critic stage, when the individual moves to
standing at times outside their faith. This stage is characterised
by the individual seeking internal meaning, understanding God
as also immanent, permitting debate and allowing apparently
contradictory aspects of faith and experience to be held at the
same time. At this stage, many people physically or emotionally
leave their church community. A fifth stage is that of the seer, a
time when contradictory aspects are harmonised, boundaries of
belief become porous, the acceptance of symbol and imagery increases, and a relish of the vastness of the unknown is experienced. A 'second naïvety' may emerge. The final stage is that of
saint, of radical 'decentralisation from self', which very few people attain.

Jamieson's focus is on why people leave churches, though
the processes he describes may be useful for identifying some of
the reasons why people in some sense stay but are attracted to
what has emerged as 'Celtic'. For many people, embracing
Celtic spirituality may be part of the process of leaving the familiar, of moving from the literalist or loyalist stages into a more
questioning form of faith, in search of greater connectivity with
other people and the opportunity to ask large questions. We see
this especially in the attractions to pilgrimage, belonging to dispersed communities and attending festivals like Greenbelt. For
people who remain formally within the churches and hope to
broaden them from within, Celtic spirituality, in particular
through its music and liturgy, makes it easier to stay. Not all do,
and Jamieson identifies one aspect of the painful 'moving on'
stage four as a period when the individual retains a Christian

faith even if they discontinue church attendance. Other aspects of this stage are a tendency to greater community commitment and social activism, and seeking the companionship of like-minded people, both of which resonate with Celtic Christianity. Following Fowler, Jamieson describes moving into the critic stage as part of a process of meeting a 'wall' and passing through it into a greater sense of freedom. This process also involves giving and receiving forgiveness. Again, the strong insistence that Celtic Christianity is a holistic faith tallies well with a stage five 'seer' approach, the period in which imagery, acceptance of new ideas, and an emphasis on harmony becomes important.

This is not the place to consider how far Fowler's and Jamieson's approaches can be usefully applied to church life in general. Certainly, people do not move automatically from stage to stage, and often retain some characteristics of previous stages in the course of their faith life. It seems, though, that the 'Stages of Faith' provide a general framework that helps to explain many of the aspects of Celtic spirituality.

While Jamieson concentrates on the faith of evangelicals, much is also applicable to those in Catholic traditions who are also drawn to the 'Celtic', as individuals and as church groups.

Many people associated with Celtic spirituality, Pagan as well as Christian, would identify themselves with the later stages of faith. If this occurs in a relatively light and self-focused way, it makes it difficult to progress to the radical movement away from self envisaged in the final stage. Indeed, a superficial concept of these later stages may fit well with an individualistic approach of seeking harmony with the surrounding world and the company of selected like-minded people. This may cause difficulty if there has been no experience of the 'conformist' stage three, as the skills of this stage are needed to hold a voluntary membership together. A vital element of church life, but arguably also of personal spiritual development, is contact with people the individual has not selected but with whom they have to work.

Most serious believers carry some traits of each stage, and if the dominant one is stage four or five, Celtic spirituality may well appeal, whether a person's faith is strong or slight. The liminality, the emphasis on the heart and their own experience, the self-selecting nature of the relationships in the formal or informal community they join, the freedom to debate faith, the ability to select aspects of various spiritual traditions, are among the elements that attract.

It has been suggested that in a post-Christian society it is not uncommon to start a personal faith journey at stage four or five, when the character is formed and intellectual exploration is united with experience.[1] A personal view is that most people using the Celtic movement are at the fourth stage, the church-leaver stage, but that there are also newcomers without a formal faith community for whom the 'Celtic' can be a way into Christianity. They may be psychologically at the fourth or even fifth stages but without a faith vocabulary, and Celtic spirituality, with its gentle accessibility, can be a means by which belief can be expressed and shared, and life experience made sense of. Either newcomers or church-leavers who are predominantly at the fourth stage and are also engaged in social activism, may find fulfilment in this expression of faith, with its critical yet broad approach to matters of belief, its acceptance of beauty and its emphasis on the immanence of God. Those at the fifth stage enjoying a 'second naïvety' may also find pleasure in returning to what is superficially the childhood literalist stage, especially in relation to storytelling. They may find some effort is needed to accommodate aspects of the earlier stages involving literal knowledge and the value of church community, but the critical and socially-active aspects of the newcomer's faith are recognised, and their life experience taken into account.

Critical explorers of faith and church-leavers are not the target audiences envisaged by the evangelical and mission-orientated writers of the 1980s and 1990s, whose intention was to speak to the 'unchurched' and invite them in. Celtic spirituality to them provided a place to start the journey of faith, but is in fact being used to address its later stages. This was recognised by some more recent writers, like John Bell and Graham Maule of the Wild Goose Worship Group, and John O'Donohue, whose appeal is largely to actual or psychological church-leavers who wish to retain and perhaps radicalise their faith.

1. Talk prepared by Linsi Simmons, Bible Society weekend on culture and the changing church, spring 2004.

If this analysis is true, and the movement is catering more for church-leavers than newcomers, we need to ask whether in its current form it is strong enough to carry the expectations placed upon it, and whether it can provide spirituality for people at the level they need. One of the tensions identified by Fowler and Jamieson is between people at these later stages of faith and the majority of church-goers who are at the third stage, where conformism and community take a high place. It is from this group that the teachers, and often ministers, are drawn. They may struggle with people coming to faith at the later, apparently uncritical and ungrounded stages, stages which may appear to ignore essential knowledge of doctrine and experience of church life. Meanwhile, newcomers at these stages may be frustrated by church officials who appear to diminish their life and spiritual experience to date, and to instruct rather than discuss. For the instructors too, some aspects of Celtic spirituality may appear to be ungrounded and undermining rather than nourishing.

However, there is recognition among the major Protestant denominations that traditional ways of organising church life are no longer attracting people, and we have considered how new approaches, such as 'Fresh Expressions', have been tried. This brings us to the possibility that not only individuals but some contemporary churches are moving into the Fowler-Jamieson stage four of faith, the critical, questioning stage which seeks to relate to people outside the traditional models, and to work in less formal ways. Celtic spirituality has a fair amount to offer to emerging forms of church, including liturgical and biblical experimentation, the networking of people in dispersed communities, and the recognition that people need to be met on their own ground.

As well as much to offer, there may also be limitations. A weakness for those who have left formal churches, especially in evangelical circles, is the limited knowledge of the classic writings of the Christian faith (Jamieson 2002, 169-70). A parallel is provided by the frequently impoverished nature of what is presented as 'Celtic'. While much of it may be of help during the process of leaving the certainties of the earlier stages of faith, it is difficult to see how Celtic Christianity in its current forms can provide sufficient sustenance for people actively exploring later stages in the faith journey. There is, as we have seen, limited awareness of the range of the resources that may enable people to reconnect with genuine, ancient or local traditions of faith. The dependence on derivative material also means a dependence on a small number of apparently authoritative writers, to whom for lack of alternatives, they may have to defer.

Another matter may be a tension for church-leavers between including everything in order not to cut anyone or anything out, something the all-embracing nature of Celtic spirituality encourages; and retaining enough tradition to provide the spiritual backbone than enables people explore resources and to grow independently.

These then are a few of the issues that Celtic spirituality raises in terms of theology and approach to Christian life. We turn now to more personal suggestions on ways the use of the Celtic can be taken forward.

CHAPTER EIGHT

Building on the local:
Suggestions for the future

It is the custom for writers of books on Celtic spirituality to make suggestions of their own on the way forward. What follows is a purely personal interpretation from a Christian perspective of the limited number of sources known to me, and coloured through the appreciation of Celtic Studies derived through the Penguin edition of Jackson's richly romantic *A Celtic Miscellany*, a collection that gives much space to nature poetry, otherworld journeys and descriptive passages from all the Celtic languages. What follows may be critiqued in the same way as other writers have been in this book and perhaps for similar reasons. Others will have different suggestions on how what is valued in the movement today may be developed in the future.

This book has been critical of the extraction of pieces to suit modern purposes without regard for the tradition and the culture which produced them. But it is in the nature of tradition that it constantly changes and adapts to suit new circumstances. This needs to occur, for unless tradition is open to change it becomes frozen and no longer relevant, neither nourishing nor unifying.

Where do we take this interest in the Celtic? Are there ways that by returning to the some of the roots, it is possible to find a synthesis, a way of using these traditions while relating to our own world and to concerns which have changed even since this phase of the Celtic started in the 1980s? Are there ways in which we can develop a positive dynamic that will spark off new ideas while using the material we have received in a manner that is in some way true to it, and in a form that can be passed on with integrity?

How do we encourage people to enjoy the sources, either as art or as prayer, and see them as relevant to them own lives? An uneasiness is expressed by many writers of the modern movement, a desire to present an 'authentic' Celtic spirituality, free from romantic accretions, an uneasiness that suggests they are aware of the limitations of the derivative material at their disposal. Are there ways to reconnect with the original material and its contexts? If the derivative aspects outbalance direct use of the sources, their attraction will pall and this will limit their chances of people using them further to move towards the centre of Christian spirituality, the relationship with Christ which the authors saw as the purpose of their writing, copying, illuminating, building and developing community.

Studying the sources

To do this, we need to give time to search in the original sources and their languages, or at the least to learn more from those who do, using their knowledge as we use the knowledge of biblical scholars to more fully understand the scriptures. Theology, in Christian terms, is loving God with the mind, a necessary corollary to the love of the heart. At present, the realities of the original texts are sometimes obscured by the Victorian translations with their romantic and primativist expectations. More recently a range of texts have been translated by academics more interested in the linguistic content rather than the subject. A demand for translations of texts with the theological content, accompanied by commentaries to help the general reader, may encourage further funding of work by sympathetic scholars. Certainly, learning from those who have worked with the original texts may draw the reader to appreciate more fully the writers who left prayers of power and beauty, but who provided the apparent spontaneity by living to a strict monastic lifestyle that gave time to prayer, work and study. The work put by contemporary readers into considering the material on its own terms may help a fuller understanding of the original vision and how it related to the ways in which they lived, and may assist with discerning what be can taken from it today.

One of the issues discussed in the previous chapter was how scholars have responded to the beauty of their sources and wished to make them available, through the labour of editing or through the skills of translation, to a wider audience. Though the results may be taken out of context, there is a limit to how much we will ever know about their original contexts, or even if we did learn more, how we could relate them to our lives in the twenty-first century.

There is one major area where it can be done. Whatever the cultural, historical and linguistic differences, most of the sources we use are conscious prayers, or are about prayer. We are not taking them out of context when they are used for this original purpose, nor dishonouring their writers, but using them essentially as they were intended, a means of communication with God, or of reflection on God. Many of them do not need adaptation, for their originality and strangeness stretches the believer to experience prayer in new ways.

Nature and the Saints

Both the 'hermit poetry' and the *Lives of the Saints* with their apparent closeness to the natural world have become very popular. It is difficult not to be moved by some of the stories and by the ancient, medieval or folk poetry in the Gaelic and Welsh languages, whether or not they are part of a continuum or are different, unconnected, expressions of the same themes. People respond to the beauty, to the balance between the strange and the familiar, and to the vivid imagery.

Perhaps we could include material not usually seen in the canon, for example the deeply religious nature poetry of poems of *Suibhne geilt* and some of the *Duanaire Finn* cycle. These poems are wrapped in a literary conceit that resonates with the current movement and its love for stories.

This must be one reason too why the *Lives of the Saints* are so popular. The image of the Celts as doing theology with imagery rather than intellectually appeals to those who attend 'Celtic Christianity' events, and the stories of the saints are often used as extended images, parables with a point. Given the biblical tradition of engaging at a deep level through parable, through story, there are strong theological reasons to support the growth of this side of the movement.

We might again try to broaden the base. For example, accounts of Saint Columba and his coming to Iona almost all cite a late story of his being a penitent, who had caused a battle in Ireland after a dispute over copyright. The story goes that he borrowed a psalter from Saint Finnian, secretly copied it and then returned the original. Finnian, having heard of the copy, demanded it too. The matter went to the judgement of the high-king, a relative of Columba, who nevertheless declared that 'to every cow its calf, to every book its copy'. Columba did not accept this verdict and the matter led to the battle of Cúl Dreimne in 561, a battle in which many died. In consequence, Columba went into exile.

The story appears in this form nearly a thousand years after the event in 1532, in a *Life of Columba* by Manus O'Donnell. This Donegal author wrote for publication in the age of print, so his interest in ownership is understandable. Further, his family preserved the *Cathach*, a psalter attributed to, and old enough to be written by, Columba. The tale may have developed to account for the psalter's name *Cathach*, 'battler', and the reported practice of carrying it three times round the O'Donnell host before combat no doubt strengthened the association.

The use of this story is likely to continue, seeing that most writers have an interest in copyright issues. But it means that we do not see what other accounts imply, a man working out of his strengths, as a member of a royal house extending the Christian message among his own people, using his innate privileges to proclaim the gospel. Though less vivid, we may have lost some richness in texture and aspects that might resonate for modern Christian mission.

Stories might help to find a place for a much underused part of the Irish tradition, the focus on one saint, the Virgin Mary. As we have seen, Mary is avoided in the Protestant works on Celtic spirituality, while even the Irish writings of John O'Donohue give her little place. Yet in vernacular religious tradition her position remains strong, and there is rarely a group of houses in rural Ireland without a grotto, a shrine commemorating her. Statues also appear at the spontaneous wayside shrines that mark traffic accidents, while the bells, though not the words, of the traditional Marian prayer *The Angelus*, are transmitted by the State broadcaster RTÉ twice a day as a 'Pause for thought'. There are regular pilgrimages from Ireland to Lourdes, Medugorje, and within Ireland to the County Mayo shrine at Knock. These vernacular Catholic practices, the strong emphasis in Ireland on the more emotive sides of her devotion, and the historical

Protestant wariness of any recognition of her role, have possibly obscured a part of the tradition we must explore if we are to be true to the whole.

Mary appears in early Irish literature most dramatically in the eighth-century lament by the poet Blathmac. She is portrayed holding Jesus in her arms on two high crosses on Iona and in the *Book of Kells* (which was believed to have been started there in the late eighth century), making them the oldest portraits of Mary in western Christian art. She is addressed in one of the earliest poems from Iona, in Latin (Markús and Clancy 1995 182-92), and reappears in folk tradition, Irish as well as Hebridean. A version of the folk lament, *Caoineadh na Maighdine*, the *Lament of the Virgin*, a medieval European lament of Mary at the foot of the Cross, is printed by James Carney in his book on *Medieval Irish Lyrics*, and a number of sung versions have been recorded in recent years.

It is possible to take the medieval and some of the folk accounts as narrative theology. Blathmac's poem, and indeed the *Lament of the Three Marys* may be addressed to the Virgin Mary, but they perceive her as a participant in events recorded in the New Testament. These poems are imaginative expressions of her grief, and that of the onlooker, who is the reciter. Both the ancient and the relatively recent folk poems retell an aspect of the Christian story, relating it to people of the reciter's own time. These laments are also in the main fine works of art, and their beauty helps the modern reciter to collaborate with the purpose of the author.

The more Protestant traditions might avoid most of the folk poetry, which directly invokes Mary. But failing to use these poems at all distorts the tradition. The modern emphasis on narrative theology, the use of the imagination, is one way to approach them. This sits well too with the Ignatian tradition of imaginative spirituality which has influenced readers from the more Catholic end of the movement. Finally, acknowledging the significance of Mary in the tradition helps us to understand certain other female saints, Bridget, and also lesser-known Irish saints like Ita, with their imagined roles as midwives to Jesus. This is a manifestation of a literary conceit also found in early Irish secular literature, that certain heroic characters were contemporaries of Christ. When used about the saints this makes a theological point that the events in the life of Jesus are from a Christian perspective universal, and Christians of all time and place can participate in them. The Christian is invited through the Marian poems to join Mary and companions, including the author, at the foot of the Cross, knowing too that the resurrection will follow.

Rediscovering English tradition
The lives of Mary and the other saints will also be found in other early traditions that could be explored further in the quest for a richer Celtic spirituality. The English tradition contains much that relates to the Virgin Mary, and in some cases a semi-vernacular tradition concerning Mary has been revived, for example the pilgrimages to Walsingham in Norfolk undertaken in the Catholic and High-Church Anglican traditions.

In exploring the English traditions, we may also find much whch is not, and need not be called 'Celtic'. The Northumbrian missionaries of the 1980s modelled themselves on the missionaries of the sixth century, Irish or English. They took what was beautiful, publicised it and adapted it for the needs of mission as they saw it. This form of Celtic spirituality might grow through rediscovering the great Anglo-Saxon religious tradition, the joyful freedom of medieval English spirituality, and the remaining English vernacular religious practices.

Some anthologies of English spirituality have appeared and this is certainly an area that could be developed, to ensure that English resources are not dependant only on reading Bede in his Northumbrian context and the other *Lives of the Saints*. There is a wealth of poetry and prayer in Old English.

Perhaps the greatest and largely overlooked contribution is the extraordinary poem, *The Dream of the Rood*, which tells the story of the Crucifixion from the perspective of the tree cut down to make the cross. The narrator addresses us directly, telling of the dream he had of seeing the cross, which then in turn becomes the narrator. Christ is depicted as a young Saxon hero battling his enemies, the forces of evil, actively placing himself on the cross, dying in order that others might live. The cross is the participator and commentator, engaged not only as a

tree but as a follower of his warlord. Both the cross and the narrator comment on the effect upon them of Christ's death and
resurrection. An added element for the modern reader is that,
like much of this tradition, *The Dream of the Rood* has survived
against the odds. The whole poem is known from a single manuscript, and part of it had been inscribed in runes on the
Ruthwell Cross in south-western Scotland, a cross that was itself
damaged but not destroyed at the Reformation.

As an example of inculturation, the Christian gospel seen
through the culture in which it was being spread, and as narrative theology, the telling of the Christian story from a new angle,
The Dream of the Rood has immense potential as a resource for
modern understanding of mission. It is exquisitely composed,
an example of the spread of Christianity through the use of art.
It uses the culture in which it was born, identifies in its greatest
themes an aspect of the universal Christ, and expresses the unity
of the two by combining the imagery through the art of poetry.

The quirky lives of the Northumbrian saints extracted from
writers like Bede are attractive, but the *Dream of the Rood*, written
in the native language of Northumbria, expresses the universal,
and tells the story of the crucifixion through the imagery of its
own time. As a great work of art *The Dream of the Rood* gives
some real understanding of the world of the English in the first
centuries of Christianity, and of the issues that concerned them,
seen through their own heroic traditions.

Other specifically religious poems can also be explored more
fully. There are other great narrative poems told in the first person, *The Seafarer* and *The Wanderer*, with their visions of the stoic
hero with his rest in Christ, poems that convey some of the most
powerful images of nature in its colder aspects, of pain, loss, the
memory of better times, all of them relevant for the explorer of
spirituality today. *The Seafarer* in particular fits in well with the
pilgrimage tradition, including pilgrimage as penitence, with its
overtones of exile. Like the Irish traditions, the Old English
poems of exile have strong biblical resonances, and while truly
'on the edge' in the sense of being alone and at sea, the narrator
is held within the unseen Christian community. The God they
address is present even when this does not bring emotional
comfort.

We may consider too the other poetry of this culture. Some of the shorter poems, including Caedmon's prayer and Bede's death-song are already well-known, but in considering the longer narratives, we might provide an awareness of the other religious poems and some, if not all, of the riddles. When introduced to these poems in translation, groups as diverse as attenders at a mental health day-care centre and professional theologians have found that they continue to speak to the human condition, and to relate the Christian story in a powerful way.

We do not need to stop with the early English. Eamon Duffy's *The Stripping of the Altars* (1999) examines in depth, and with much sensitive humour, late-medieval English Catholic practice. Seasons, saints, place and pilgrimage figure prominently, and he includes both actual prayers of the period and pictures of the visual art it produced. The reluctance of the populace, the 'common people' to lose their traditions at the Reformation is dealt with at length. His work is not referred to in books about Celtic Christianity, yet it contains material on themes loved by the movement. Duffy provides the references by which people can delve into the corpus of medieval English religious poetry and prose, and in spite of the language difficulties learn to enjoy the riches that are a genuine part of native English heritage. While the number of mellifluous prayers that have survived are not as plentiful as the Hebridean harvest, practices are described that relate to these prayers, and the basis is provided for new compositions. Themes that can be derived from his work include those related to the seasons, and the changing nature of how we get our food and at what cost to whom. These tie in directly with modern concerns on the nature of trade, the distribution of wealth, access to good health, and the effects of climate change on the poorest. Similarly, the medieval English saints he refers to are as eclectic as those provided by Celtic spirituality. While most readers may not wish to invoke them, their stories provide food for thought and characters to emulate. The places of pilgrimage similarly might provide for the fervour of locals and to some extent they are already doing so.

Duffy's work has become popular in other circles in part because he has collected some of the surviving native English poetry of celebration. It may be little known to the Celtic spirituality movement in England because of its evidently Catholic tone, but there may be ways of developing his themes, and supplementing his material from what remains of the seasonal popular tradition, gathered in collections such as Christina Hole's *A Dictionary of British Folk Customs* (1976), and the material also relevant to England in Kevin Danagher's *The Year in Ireland* (1972).

We have taken Celtic material not only from the early medieval 'Dark Ages' but also at times from the later, more Europeanised, high medieval period. We might wish to explore this further and consider the English lyrical tradition, much of which is specifically religious. Another aspect of the medieval English tradition is its group of mystical works. Four fourteenth-century classics have survived, three by authors known by name, Julian of Norwich, Richard Rolle, Walter Hilton, while the fourth author wrote *The Cloud of Unknowing*. Less elevated but more rumbustious and with some real insights is the spiritual autobiography of a businesswoman, the *Life of Margery Kempe*, which survived in a single manuscript rediscovered in the 1930s. Margery and her older contemporary Julian may provide a female balance in a literary world where most writers were anonymous but almost certainly male. Another aspect of English tradition may be a re-appreciation of the medieval architecture of the churches, and occasionally the wall-paintings rediscovered under the plaster of the Reformation period.

Returning to the older traditions of both islands, we may consider if we can make more use of their art, in particular the great Gospel books, in a visual society.

The artistic traditions
One of the advantages of modern technology means that texts and pictures can be copied, projected or otherwise used in new ways. The opportunities to use good quality reproductions provides a previously unimaginable scope in the field of art.

The twentieth century became an artistically visual society, one used to the moving image, through the use of film and later television. At the same time there has been increased appreciation in religious circles, Protestant as well as the Catholic, of the art of previous ages, and in particular, the spirituality of the icons of the eastern Orthodox tradition.

Most of the history of Christianity is of societies where books were rare and were more likely to be heard than privately read. As a result, much of the interpretation of the scriptures was done by our ancestors through visual means, through works of art in churches, and through illustrations, illuminations, of handwritten religious books. Many of the tools for interpreting the visual were lost in the west in the centuries after the Reformations, which were dominated by the printed word. However, in recent times scholarly works have appeared that help us to understand something of the subtlety of the art of the great Gospel books. Work of people like Janet Backhouse on the *Lindisfarne Gospels* and Carol Farr and others on the *Book of Kells* can show to a society that enjoys the visual and is accustomed to symbolism in pictorial art, how to appreciate these works again.

The *Book of Kells* is perhaps particularly useful in terms of Celtic spirituality, for although much damaged it contains a number of full-page illuminations which can be treated as icons. Some of these may at first sight seem crudely drawn and alien, while the more abstract pages may seem to be no more than enthusiastic doodles which give delight to the eye with their richness of colour and attention to details, but not much else. This was the initial experience of a twelfth-century writer, Giraldus Cambrensis, Geoffrey of Wales, who came to Ireland with the Norman invaders and saw a similar Gospel book in Kildare. Often a hostile reporter on Irish matters, he wrote:

> Among all the miracles of Kildare nothing seems more to me more miraculous than that wonderful book which they say was written at the dictation of an angel during the lifetime of the virgin [Bridget].
>
> This book contains the concordance of the four gospels according to Saint Jerome, with almost as many drawings as pages, and all of them in marvellous colours. Here you can look upon the face of the divine majesty, drawn in a miraculous way; here too upon the mystical representations of the Evangelists, now having six, now four, and now two, wings. Here you will see the eagle, there the calf. Here the face of a man; there that of a lion. And there are almost innumerable drawings. If you look at them carelessly and casually and not

too closely, you may judge them to be mere daubs rather than careful compositions. You will see nothing subtle where everything is subtle. But if you take the trouble to look very closely, and penetrate with your eyes to the secrets of the artistry, you will notice such intricacies, so delicate and sub- tle, so close together and well-knitted, so involved and bound together, and so fresh still in their colourings that you will not hesitate to declare that these things must have been the result of the work, not of men but of angels. (1982, 84.)

Visiting the *Book of Kells* or other of the Gospel books today is a tourist experience rather than a liturgical or meditative one, but through technology we have the same opportunity to view the detail of the artwork in other surroundings. We are learning to 'read' again the illuminations through the passages of the scriptures which inspired them. Even some of the delightful animal drawings that intersperse the text can have more signifi- cance than originally appears.

This might be an area where Celtic spirituality might grow, through the use of art to interpret the scriptures, and by enjoy- ment of the sheer exuberance of the Gospel books. This brings us back to the hermeneutics of beauty, to the freshness of dis- covery, and provides opportunities for seeing with new eyes in a manner ideal for a society used to the visual. Other texts such as the *Lindisfarne Gospels* also lend themselves to attention to detail, detail sometimes too small for most people to see, pro- duced by the monastic scribes of more than a millennium ago.

For this we need scholarly help with understanding the meaning, so as to feed the popular and the devotional. As this is a relatively untouched field, it might also be a helpful one for practitioners of the movement to re-evaluate the fear that the academic world is dry, closed and dismissive of the pleasure people find in Celtic spirituality.

Another area in which we might be able to connect Celtic spirituality with other fields is that of folk music. The end of the twentieth century saw an upsurge in interest in traditional music, an upsurge which, in spite of the interest of hymns and liturgy in the Celtic movement, seems not to have touched any area of Christian spirituality. Commercial tapes of reflective music are indeed often used in devotional settings, but there has been little direct contact between the two movements and live performances of traditional music in liturgy are rare. There have been some liturgical experiments, where traditional religious songs have been used in different settings, the best known of which is the collaboration between the traditional singer Nóirín Ní Riain and the monks of Glenstal abbey in County Limerick who sing Gregorian chant.

We might explore if there are also matters of process that could be helpful to spiritual engagement. One of the delights of a live 'session' is the commitment of the players to quality, and another is the willingness of the more experienced to carry the novice musicians. Other pleasures include the blending of various instruments and the ways in which different players can lead on different tunes, set the tempo, pick up if something goes astray and redirect it, and provide the decoration and variation that keep traditional tunes alive and developing. Celtic spirituality might receive from the use of the music, while a traditional session, where different musicians take this lead role at different times, conscious of support and variety, provides lessons in teamwork from which many religious bodies could receive much.

We have considered then how we can use the fruits of study to develop in new ways aspects of the wider tradition. We may now turn to ways in which our use of the 'Celtic' may provide for modern concerns.

A planet in crisis – loving our environment

We have seen that one of the attractions of the early Christian nature poetry is that it speaks to us of matters that are burning issues today, the environment and its stewardship. Modern Celtic spirituality keeps the beauty of the world in mind and the nature poetry can be read as aids to maintaining this beauty in which God is immanent. The ways in which the natural world is treated can be directly related to how God is treated.

There is a major scriptural source for delight in and reverence for the creation, the Book of Psalms, and especially the psalms that praise God through the natural world. Celtic nature poetry is deeply influenced by the psalms, which the writers recited daily, alone or in community with others. The later, local, folk poems are often seen as a parallel form of expression of the presence of God in nature, a means of relating through the 'Book of Nature', to the 'Book of God', the scriptures.

As the effect becomes more apparent in the cost to everyone, but especially to the world's poor, of environmental damage and change, this aspect of Celtic spirituality is likely to grow. Indeed, if it does not, there must be questions about the validity and relevance of the whole movement as a path to the divine. The asceticism of the early saints might lead to some adherents adopting an environmentally less taxing lifestyle, though total emulation might be considered inadvisable. From a theological point of view, if the nature poems can raise consciousness about how we treat the world and our neighbour, they are potentially a tool of the divine, even if the way we use them today would have been incomprehensible to the original composers. There is also the possibility that our use of them will broaden their readership and their influence, which might assist the Celtic spirituality movement to move from a focus on personal self-development towards extending its role as a tool for a wider relationship between God and humanity.

Those attracted to the movement are inclined to be among those who are attempting to live in a manner sensitive to the environment, practising recycling, supporting fair trade, and engaging in activities and networks that may be influential in the wider society. The 'Celtic' may be a means of making the connections between the actions of individuals and the health of the planet, giving ancient sources a new relevance.

These suggestions are not alternatives to active responses to the crisis or to changing western lifestyles to a less wasteful mould. This book was completed during a severely cold spell in the winter of 2009-2010, when the temperatures in the west of Ireland fell to unprecedented lows, when normal life was interrupted by freezing fog and heavy snowfalls. There were shortages of tap water, and roads, schools and businesses were closed. A few weeks previously, the country had been hit by severe floods after massive rainfall. Some people suffered considerable hardship, but these problems were for most an inconvenience rather than the matter of life and death they can be in much of the world. But they showed locally how we have damaged our world globally.

Loving our neighbour –penitence and justice

Mainstream Christian theology speaks of the stewardship of the earth and the human requirement to tend it and return it to God, a tending that makes the earth flourish and give of its fruits, providing food and other essentials to life. The earth and its creatures were created by God who saw that they were very good, and humanity in its first innocence was part of this, and also very good. The provision for human need was not envisaged as harming the earth, while the surplus allowed humans to have time to enjoy life and rest in it as well as to work for food and shelter. While the population has increased hugely, as the Iona Community has expressed it, there is enough for the need of all but not for the greed of a few. Western society, willingly or not, comprises the greedy few.

We have seen how the nature poems of Celtic spirituality speak to our innate sense of connection to the natural world and our response to its beauty. But a coherent spiritual response to environmental destruction to which people can relate seems to be nearly as absent as international agreement on how to change our ways of living. There may be resources within the Celtic that can be of help if used as part of a wider, international, change of heart and direction.

While the emphasis on the goodness of creation has been very helpful at a time of increasing ecological crisis, it has always been seen as part of the natural development of the Christian spirit to become increasingly aware of sinfulness. We also saw the early Irish approach, that penance was medicine for the cure of the soul, something by extension good not only for the individual but also for society. The penitential traditions were a major part of the early tradition, and they might be of general use in a theology of restoration.

Traditionally, times of regular Christian penance included Lent and to a lesser extent Advent, seasons at which the whole of society was involved. Rich as well as poor underwent the same rigours over food and limiting their social and sexual activities. These periods were part of the rhythm of the year and the patterns of the seasons. They were times of restriction which were followed by times of celebration. What is natural in the rhythms of the year may also be natural for humans, and they provide a time to assess oneself and to cut back on behaviour that can control us. The fact that others are going through similar experiences could feed into the contemporary Celtic spirituality's desire for community-building. The early church writers took the patterns of fasting for granted, and in the western world Lent was an ideal time to fast, when food stocks, especially of meat, were getting low, when the cows had dried up and the hens stopped laying. Lent and Advent are now little observed in western Christian society, but the Muslim observance of Ramadan might give impetus to practice of the Christian equivalent.

There are other aspects that might be worth exploring in terms of community. The early sources provide the image of whole communities of penitents living together, having the benefit of each other, and also having the experience of having something to aim for – personal healing which allowed each member to eventually return to the wider community, a model not vastly different from a modern rehabilitation centre, but perhaps having a wider relevance. Members of these communities, like the hermits on their rocky islands, presumably prayed for those left behind, for their family unit from whom they received their identity. The penitent, hermit, pilgrim or missionary was engaged in specialised work, away from home, as an exile for Christ, but with the opportunity in time to return as full members.

The most severe punishment for a free person was to be exiled, to become an outlaw, a kinless person, in effect a non-person, outside the system, the land and the people from which came his identity. The early Irish who became hermits or monks, whether on a rock in the sea or far away in a continental monastery, were exiles for the love of God. They took on themselves the position being through sin a criminal against God, and taking on the penalty of exile. This was the penalty for one who was a free person not a slave, in the biblical as well as the legal sense. Freely taking upon oneself the status of the criminal, to unite oneself to Jesus crucified with criminals, was also potentially a recognition of both sinfulness and redemption, an acknowledgement that the exile could be cured. Most of them also had the advantage, not available to the outlawed man, of companionship on the journey.

From this, modern readers may be able to extract a sense of the Christian life as one which involves welcoming others and serving them, even when living in isolation. Sacrifice, in Christian terms, in penitence or for other reasons, is expected to contain the joyful, to be an expression of love, a cause of hope, initiated through faith. If the modern Celtic tradition can be used to expressed the joy it is said the poetry confers, and if privations can be endured today in response to a sense of personal or social sin, most particularly in the case of the environment, this could be a positive use of ancient resources, even if one very far from the original perception, not Celtic in normal sense, but taking inspiration from the actions of an earlier society.

At the same time, on the more personal than social level, we may also wish to stay with the modern derivations of the *anamchara*, the soul-friend as listener and adviser and spiritual friend rather than anything sterner.

The penitential tradition in its personal form has much to offer, and the social applications even more, though there is little connection with the original purposes and uses other than the inspiration they provide. Another way of applying the inspiration to our own society may concern the social code and the laws and their breaking.

The penitentials were developed from ancient law codes, which continued to exist and be used, but which could be turned on their head in the spiritual context. They propose at times the lightest penalties for sin for those at the bottom of society. If we used this approach in a modern context, legal or personal, it would require us to give consideration both to the disadvantages a lawbreaker had experienced in life, but also to their advantages, with the penalties more severe for those who have received most from society. Rather than taking a retributive approach, we might use the analogy of medicine to do this in a manner that focuses on the offender's need to change by undertaking appropriate reparation. While this is suggested in terms of church and community life, it links to the developing modern approach to restorative justice. A particular insight from the Celtic perspective, developed in a society as brutal as the more disadvantaged parts of our own, is the extent to which the wider family was involved in the penalties and rehabilitation of the lawbreaker, a

social system that might need to be extended today to incorporate support from a person's work and social networks, or their
neighbourhood. It would require the commitment to support
from the believing community, but if Celtic Christianity is indeed a gentle, inclusive spirituality, a response that considers
restoration, backed by the support of others, might show the extent to which it can be radical in ordinary lives.

These are some suggestions concerning the more transfer-
able aspects of the sources, approaches which may broaden the
base of the movement. We now turn to different ways of using
the movement, for what it can offer directly for us today.

Building on the local

As well as study of the past, a way to ground the movement
may be by looking more at what people actually do and express
in the places in which they work and worship, or have done
until recently. It may prove possible to develop the 'sense of
place' by asking people about their remaining traditions and
practices.

In England the process of 'recovering' tradition pre-supposes
its having been obscured for many centuries, but in Ireland, in
both Catholic and Protestant circles, the emphasis is on the
maintenance of a tradition and its potential for spiritual resur-
gence, especially for those living in new towns and places that
are perceived as spiritually dislocated.

Various approaches have been taken to develop ecumenically a
recognition of the heritage, and of modern Celtic spirituality, that
could engage residents, incomers and visitors in new ways. Many
ancient holy places are significant to people, both locals and visitors, for a variety of reasons, which include the burial of the dead,
resting places on walks, and tourist destinations. The sites are regarded as interconnected and were memorably termed by one
commentator the 'Celtic carpet'. Many of these sacred spaces are
in the care of one of the churches or the government Office of
Public Works, and are in some sense open to everyone.

Pilgrimage and a sense of place are central to current ecumenical church thinking. Connecting with the past, with a national
heritage that can be shared with the indigenous post-Christian
population, rich and poor, has been seen in many places as es-

sential for genuine spiritual growth. Pilgrimage is something that is open to local people, to transitory visitors and to urban dwellers seeking something different. It is recognised that there need to be ways of gaining access and of using tradition in a manner acceptable to local people; and to affirm a level of spirituality, local and contemporary as well as ancient, that provides the authenticity and respect essential for the sites and their continuing local usage. 'Holistic' Celtic spirituality may be a tool that can be developed to accommodate these strands.

As we have seen, in the repeated interpretations of ancient places like Iona, the understanding of newcomers has dominated. It is necessary to respect, if not accept, what a place might mean to local people. They are not the only people whose views count, but they are the most likely to serve as the custodians.

There are differing opinions on how ancient monastic centres might be the centre of spiritual activity, but there is an acceptance of the need for 'real' input from those with the skills to interpret the sites. In the west of Ireland there are slowly developing, in different ways in different areas, prayer walks that often follow old routes between high crosses, over old boundaries, taking in ruined churches and round towers, exploring also the beauty of the land which has been farmed for millennia. On such pilgrim walks it has proved possible to use the prayers of the past but also the physical remains and the related traditions of the inhabitants down the centuries as places to pause for reflection. A discipline of preparation has been needed, of learning from scholarship, and also of discovering ways in which to break open the fruits of this study for others to share. Walking is a good way of meeting and talking to new people and pilgrimage provides for people to offer their skills, knowledge, and ability to entertain. Storytelling has proved effective, the telling of ancient stories of how others have lived in the places encountered, connecting them to the scriptures, which were known to those to whom these places were sacred, and also to more personal stories and reflections on contemporary situations. The visiting of places holy since ancient times, and still regarded as holy through the visits of praying people down the centuries, has combined with the use, mainly in translation, of ancient prayers, some older than the ruined buildings themselves. The walks also pass places honoured by local people, including grottos and wayside shrines which also mark cultural and theological boundaries.

This approach is suited to our own times and interpretations of what we see, the ruins and also the farmed landscape and settlement patterns of generations which have left signs of their own beliefs and way of life. The ruins themselves replaced older structures, and before Christianity were generations of other inhabitants. Even with the help of archaeologists, historians, and the often well-informed builders of the Office of Public Works who stabilise these structures, we may be imposing our own views as much as the eighteenth-century travellers to Iona imposed their own interpretations on the ruins they saw. We need to see them through our own eyes to enjoy them, but we need to distinguish between what belongs to known fact and what is our own.

Not all modern practices have been acceptable. To some local people, walking to and praying at ancient sites may appear as at best another fad, at worst an imposition of the experience of others. Expressions like 'Claiming Clare for Christ' are standard in some strands of Christianity, but are seen as aggression, of colonisation by others. In turn, some evangelical Christians have reservations about 'rounds', the traditional walked prayers associated with holy sites. The traditional practice is very Catholic in the content of the prayers, but walking through prescribed patterns of movement is not so different from the modern 'prayer labyrinth'. Other practices may be distinctive only in their purpose, for the focus of the walks is likely to be on pilgrimage, but many routes between historical sites have been signed for walkers.

Themes that have been commonly used in prayer walking have been those that address contemporary needs, often in images brought to mind by the scenery and ruins visited. In recent times they have included, as recession has bitten, the parables of Jesus that identify human relationships as the true focus when handling money. The survivors of institutions where children were abused, those who sit in the sun until the eleventh hour because there is no work, those who have lost family to traffic accidents, farmers working in a changing climate, have all been recalled. In a land whose national catastrophe was the Great Famine, there is a recognition of the places in the world where the harvest has failed; and in a landscape full of the ruins not only of monasteries but of castles, of the need for peace in world politics today. The scenery, and the plants, butterflies, birds have led to prayers for the stewardship of the earth to prevent catastrophic climate change. Walkers have tried to move away from congratulating themselves for being on the margins, to focus on the people who have been put on margins, the stranger, the economic migrant, the people who have remained poor through the time of wealth, and the people who centred their lives on work, homes and holidays, and have lost them.

Whether this approach is 'Celtic' or not, it is one contemporary way which seeks to honour the heritage in stone and writings, in farming and faith, in storytelling and silent prayer, in travelling to holy places, and to using what has been received for the common journey. There are many other ways, and each country and each culture will have its own variety. But it has seemed in this practice that the best heritage of the 'Celtic' is to reconnect people to the place and culture in which they find themselves, to honour the past by discovering it again, perhaps at some cost to their expectations, and to honour the present in ways that enrich relationships to each other and to the wider world. It is not particular to any culture or time, though the prayers used may be, and in doing this in one place it may be possible to rediscover the wonder and delight that has passed down through the centuries in words, art and buildings.

Owning without possessing: stewardship without domination
This practice has grown in part because it is seen as on the edge, liminal. It leaves the question of who owns the heritage, the land, the texts, or indeed who owns Celtic spirituality.

A much-quoted story mentioned earlier gives a reason for Columba's founding the monastery on Iona. In this apocryphal tale he had borrowed and then secretly copied a psalter. We are not told whose copy was copied in the first place or how far back this judgement should go, but much of this book has been about the ownership of texts. In spite of the quest for wildness, simplicity and being on the edge in Celtic spirituality, there are still questions about what is owned and by whom. The original owners, the authors or copyists are long since gone. Do the scholars own the texts they have preserved, edited, translated and brought before a wider but still specialist public? Do the writers of the modern movement who have seized upon, enjoyed, reinterpreted, bowdlerised or published as fact, own their works, which others in turn copy? Do the poets like David Adam writing in the Celtic tradition own the tradition? Do the audience, who read and enjoy the texts, own Celtic spirituality? Do the native Gaelic speakers and Welsh speakers and their descendants own the products of their traditions? Are they owned by the followers of the English version of Celtic spirituality, who can enjoy it in their own language and culture today? Do the sources belong to the countries of the Celtic fringe? Or do we all at some level, and often simultaneously, own it? If so, we also have the responsibility of stewardship. It matters how we use what we have inherited, and how we interpret, reference, harvest what we like, and leave as much as possible of the tradition for the future to make sense of in its own ways. Rigorous research on the sources need not be a threat to the movement, or an attempt to diminish the real spiritual contribution modern Celtic spirituality has made, but it is a privilege as much as a right to work with what has been received from the past, and a matter of essential respect to give the best interpretations we can if we are to honour the writers and their art.

To own in any sense can, and perhaps should, involve care and stewardship for something inanimate. It is not necessarily a one-to-one exchange. We can own something communally or at different levels, depending on our responsibility. The land on which we walk is owned by people who live on it, and the farmers who have the most intense caring relationship with it, but the land is also owned in some sense by the wider society, and in another by those who love it, by the people who have walked on it, and by those who have been forced to leave but love it in memory or through descendants who value it. It was owned before us by the people who farmed it in the past and passed it on to us, most of them unknown. The future generations have a right to ownership in turn of what we have loved.

Engagement, responsibility and stewardship, whether for land, historic sites, ancient texts or folk tradition can occur at different levels. We can all have some ownership, as long as it respects the level to which others are engaged, as long as stewardship and care are present, as long as the past is respected and the future provided for.

We can see it in the ways in which people of different cultures and ages have found pleasure in the all the aspects that attract us. More, Celtic spirituality has not been the province of any single creed or denomination within Christianity, but has spoken to people across the different traditions. Parallels can be seen in how the original scriptures on which Christianity is based passed between countries in the international, fluid language of Latin, but from an early period in Ireland they were supplemented by writings in the local, native, language. This brought a freshness, a local element, and allowed other aspects of the native culture to be preserved and passed down for others to enjoy. When there was contact through Christian mission with other cultures such as the Anglo-Saxon, the local native language was again used as a tool for writing, for expression of the culture, and produced great works like *The Dream of the Rood*.

Another image can be drawn from the history of some of the great Gospel books in England. Written in Latin, the earliest might come from Ireland or Iona, or may have been written locally by scribes schooled by teachers from the Gaelic world. We know in the case of one such book, *MacRegol's Gospels*, that it was written in Ireland, but crossed the water and in time had Old English translations written between the lines of the Latin text. Over the centuries we can point to other parts of the cultural heritage, that were re-translated for the people of their time.

We can even note that what we call Celtic spirituality is now almost entirely transmitted in English, the language derived from Anglo-Saxon, the language now dominant in Ireland, and in a simplified form used internationally as Latin once was. We can see too how the international language of art has been re-interpreted for different periods. We can trace how our understanding of Celtic spirituality has changed down the centuries until it found its modern form. Perhaps by our partial ownership and certain stewardship, there may be ways in which the Celtic can contribute in new ways across the divides of history and culture.

Finally

We now have more access than ever before to the prayers of the written or popular traditions of the last fifteen hundred years. As more and more appears on the internet, these opportunities will increase, as will our need to sift and make the material manageable. Some of the themes of Celtic Christianity are in fact universal: the turn of the seasons; the nature of daily work; the ages of human life; the harmony and interconnectedness of the universe; and the duty to provide for the traveller. Contemporary society, for all its perceived post-modern fragmentation, seems to feel the need to explore these aspects of human life as much as our ancestors did, and this need has been fed by the 'Celtic'. The use of the poetry, stories and artwork may be seen as relating to the divine through ancient material known in modern adaptations. The relationship is richest where the people who bring them have been faithful to their originals and have left markers to help us find the springs from which they drew.

While we want to belong to contemporary society, we also want a sense of wildness, a place on the edge where our individuality may find expression. In a life of faith, a productive tension between the two may be experienced. For many, this may be part of the attraction to the 'Celtic'. The material appeals to the deep sense of romance that makes us people who can react to the spiritual. Behind all the quirks of the current movement we catch glimpses of a real yearning for that which is beyond.

Celtic spirituality is wild but safe. It appeals to twentieth-century Christians with a conscience. It remains within contemporary Christianity, although its adherents may sit lightly to traditional church organisation.

'Celtic' to most modern readers means all that is delightful, natural, marginal and relational. It may not be true – but it works. If it contained more truth, it might work better. This may be the challenge of the texts we enjoy so much.

Works cited

1. REFERENCE WORKS, HISTORICAL TEXTS AND PRE-1980 ANTHOLOGIES

Adamnán of Iona, *Life of St Columba*, trs Richard Sharpe, Harmondsworth, 1991.

Bede, *Ecclesiastical History of the English People*, trs Leo Sherley-Price, revised R. E. Latham, Harmondsworth, 2001.

Blathmac, *The Poems of Blathmac Son of Cú Brettan,* ed James Carney, Dublin, 1964.

Buile Suibhne ... The Adventures of Suibhne Geilt, ed J. G. O'Keefe, London, 1913.

Carmichael, Alexander, *Carmina Gadelica*, 6 vols, Edinburgh, 1900-71.

—, *Carmina Gadelica,* Edinburgh, 1992 (English texts).

—, *The Sun Dances*, selected Adam Bittleston, Edinburgh, 1960.

__, *New Moon of the Seasons*, selected Michael Jones, Edinburgh, 1986.

Carney, James, *Medieval Irish Lyrics*, 1967. Reprinted with *The Irish Bardic Poet*, Dublin, 1985.

Davies, Oliver and Fiona Bowie eds *Celtic Christian Spirituality: An Anthology of Medieval and Modern Sources*, London, 1995.

Dwelly, Edward, *The Illustrated Gaelic-English Dictionary*, 1901-11. Reprinted Glasgow, 1977.

Farmer, D. H. ed, *The Age of Bede*, trs J. F. Webb, Harmondsworth, 1965.

Giraldus Cambrensis, Gerald of Wales, *The history and topography of Ireland*, trs John O'Meara. Revised edition, Harmondsworth. 1982.

Greene, David and Frank O'Connor, *A Golden Treasury of Irish Poetry, AD 600-1200*, London, 1967. Reprinted Brandon, 1990.

Hull, Eleanor, ed, *The Poem-Book of the Gael*, London, 1913.

Hyde, Douglas (de hÍde, Dubhglas), *Amhráin Diadha Chúige Chonnacht: The Religious Songs of Connacht*, 2 vols, London, Dublin, 1906.

Jackson, Kenneth, *Studies in Early Celtic Nature Poetry*, Cambridge, 1935.

Jackson, Kenneth, *A Celtic Miscellany*, London, 1951. Revised Harmondsworth, 1971.

Kennedy-Fraser, Marjory, *Songs of the Hebrides*, London, 1909.

MacLean, G. R. D., *Poems of the Western Highlanders*, Edinburgh, 1961.

MacLennan, Malcolm, *A Pronouncing and Etymological Dictionary of the Gaelic Language*, Edinburgh, 1925. Reprinted Aberdeen 1979, 1982.

Macleod, Fiona [William Sharp], *From the Hills of Dream: Threnodies, Songs and Later Poems*, London, 1907.

—, *Iona*, London, 1910, Edinburgh, 1982, 1991.

McNeill, F. Marian, *An Iona Anthology*, Edinburgh, 1947. Revised Glasgow, 1952.

MacPherson, James, *The Poems of Ossian, the Son of Fingal*, 2 vols, Translated from the Galic Language by T. Becky and P. A. Dehondet, 1765, 3rd ed. First published 1760.

Márkus, Gilbert, and Thomas Clancy, *Iona: the Earliest Poetry of a Celtic Monastery*, Edinburgh, 1995.

Márkus, Gilbert, *Adamnán's 'Law of the Innocents'*, Glasgow, 1997.

Meyer, Kuno, *Selections from Ancient Irish Poetry*, London, 1911.

Murphy, Gerard, *Early Irish Lyrics*, Oxford, 1956.

O'Connor, Frank, *A Book of Ireland*, Glasgow, 1959.

Ó Fiannachta, Pádraig and Desmond Forristal, *Saltair: Urnaithe duchais: Prayers from the Irish tradition*, Dublin, 1988.

Ó Laoghaire, Diarmuid, *Ár bPaidreacha Dúchais*, Dublin, 1982.

Plummer, Charles, *Lives of the Irish Saints*, 2 vols, Oxford, 1922.

Stokes, Whitley, ed, *Lives of the Saints from the Book of Lismore*, Oxford, 1890.

Uí Bhraonáin, Donla, ed, *Paidreacha na Gaelige: Prayers in Irish*, Baile Átha Cliath (Dublin), 2008.

De Waal, Esther, *The Celtic Vision: Prayers and Blessings from the Outer Hebrides. Selections from the Carmina Gadelica*, London, 1988.

Waddell, Helen, *Medieval Latin Lyrics*, Harmondsworth, 1929.

2. SECONDARY ACADEMIC WORKS

Allchin, A. M., *Celtic Christianity, Fact or Fantasy?* Bangor, 1993.

Atherton, Mark, ed, *Celts and Christians: New Approaches to the Religious Traditions of Britain and Ireland*, Cardiff, 2002.

—, 'Introduction', in Atherton ed 2002, 1-16.

Blair, John, *The Church in Anglo-Saxon Society*, Oxford, 2005.

Backhouse, Janet, *The Lindisfarne Gospels*, Oxford, 1981.

Bowman, Marion. 'More of the Same? Christianity, Vernacular Religion and Alternative Spirituality in Glastonbury,' in *Beyond the New Age: Exploring Alternative Spirituality*, eds Steven Sutcliffe and Marion Bowman, Edinburgh, 2000, 83-104.

—, 'Procession and Possession in Glastonbury: Continuity, Change and the Manipulation of Tradition', *Folklore* 115 (2004), 273-85.

Brown, Dauvit, and Thomas Clancy, eds, *Spes Scotorum: Hope of Scots. Saint Columba, Iona and Scotland*, Edinburgh, 1999.

Carey, John, *A Single Ray of the Sun*, Andover/Aberystwyth, 1999.

—, *King of Mysteries*, Dublin, 2000.

Cavill, Paul, *Anglo-Saxon Christianity*, London, 1999

Christian, Jessica, and Charles Stiller, *Iona Portrayed: The Island Through Artists' Eyes, 1760-1960*, Inverness, 2000.

Corning, Caitlin, *The Celtic and Roman traditions: conflict and consensus in the early medieval church*, New York/Basingstoke, 2006.

Dales, Douglas, *Light to the Isles: Missionary theology in Celtic and Anglo Saxon Britain*, Cambridge, 1997.

Davies, Oliver, *Celtic Christianity in early medieval Wales: the Origins of the Welsh Spiritual Tradition*, Cardiff, 1996.

Dillon, Miles, ed, *Early Irish Society*, Cork, 1954, 1963.

Etchingham, Colmán, *Church organisation in Ireland, AD 650 to 1000*, Maynooth, 1999.

Farr, Carol, *The Book of Kells: its function and audience*, London, 1997.

Hardinge, Leslie, *The Celtic Church in Britain*, London, 1972.

Harrington, Christina, *Women in a Celtic Church: Ireland 450-1150*, Oxford, 2002.

Herbert, Máire, *Iona, Kells and Derry: the history and hagiography of the monastic Familia of Columba*, Dublin, 1988. Revised 1996.

Herrin, Michael W. and Shirley Ann Brown, *Christ in Celtic Christianity: Britain and Ireland from the Fifth to the Tenth Century*, Woodbridge, 2002.

Hughes, Kathleen and Ann Hamlin, *The Modern Traveller to the Early Irish Church*, London, 1977.

Hutton, Ronald, *The Druids*, London, Continuum, 2007.

Low, Mary, *Celtic Christianity and Nature: Early Irish and Hebridean Traditions*, Edinburgh, 1996.

Mackey, James, ed, *An Introduction to Celtic Christianity*, Edinburgh, 1989.

Mackey, James, 'Is there a Celtic Christianity?', in Mackey ed 1989, 1-21.

McCone, Kim, *Pagan Past and Christian Present in Early Irish Literature*, Maynooth, 2000.

MacInnes, John, *Preface to Carmina Gadelica*, Edinburgh, 1992, 7-18.

Meek, Donald, 'Between faith and folklore: twentieth-century interpretations and images of Columba', in Brown and Clancy ed 1999, 253-70.

—, *The Quest for Celtic Christianity*, Edinburgh, 2000.

Ó Corráin, Donnchadh, 'Early Irish Hermit Poetry?', in Ó Corráin, Liam Breatnach, and Kim McCone, eds, *Sages, Saints and Storytellers: Celtic Studies in Honour of Professor James Carney*, Maynooth, 1989.

Ó Duinn, Seán, *Orthaí Cosanta sa chráifeacht Cheilteach*, Maigh Nuad (Maynooth), 1990.

O'Laoghaire, Diarmuid, 'Prayers and Hymns in the Vernacular', in Mackey ed 1989, 268-304.

O'Loughlin, Thomas, (2000a) *Celtic Theology: Humanity, World and God in Early Irish Writings*, London/New York, 2000.

—, *Discovering Saint Patrick*, London, 2005.

Power, Rosemary, 'A Place of Community: 'Celtic' Iona and Institutional Religion', *Folklore* 117 (2006), 33-53.

—, *The Celtic Metaphor: an expression of western Christianity in the twenty-first century?* Unpublished Research Thesis, University of Nottingham, 2008.

Richter, Michael, *The Formation of the Medieval West*, Dublin, 1994.

Sharpe. *See* Adomnnán

Tolkien, J. R. R. 'English and Welsh', in *Angles and Britons*, ed, Henry Lewis, The O'Donnell Lectures, Cardiff 1963.

Waddell, Helen, *The Wandering Scholars*, London, 1927.

Beasts and Saints, London: Constable, 1934. Edited by Esther de Waal, London, 1995.

3. BOOKS FROM THE CONTEMPORARY MOVEMENT

Abbey Services of the Iona Community, Leaflets, Iona Community, c. 1947-69.

Adam, David, *The Edge of Glory: Prayers in the Celtic Tradition*, London, 1985.

—, *The Cry of the Deer: Meditations on the Hymn of St Patrick*, London, 1987.

—, *Power lines: Celtic Prayers about Work*, London, 1992.

—, *The Fire of the North: The Illustrated Life of St Cuthbert*, London, 1993.

—, *A Celtic Daily Prayer Companion*, London, 1997.

—, *A Desert in the Ocean*, London, 2000.

—, *The Eye of the Eagle: Meditations on the Hymn 'Be Thou My Vision'*, London, 2001.

Allchin, Donald and Esther de Waal, *Threshold of Light: Poems and Prayers from the Celtic Tradition*, London, 1986.

Allchin, A. M., *God's Presence Makes the world: the Celtic vision through the centuries in Wales*, London, 1997.

Bradley, Ian, *The Celtic Way*, London, 1993.

—, *Columba, Pilgrim and Penitent*, Glasgow, 1996.

—, *Celtic Christianity: Making Myths and chasing Dreams*, Edinburgh, 1999.

—, *Colonies of heaven: Celtic Models for today's Church,* London, 2000.

Bragg, Melvyn, *Credo*, London, 1996.

Cattanach, D. L. 'St Columba and Whithorn', *Coracle* 2 (1939): 12-14.

The Coracle, Iona Community Publications 1938-

Clancy, Pádraigín, ed, *Celtic Threads*, Dublin, 1999.

Condren, Mary, *The Serpent and the Goddess: Women, Religion and Power in Celtic Ireland*, San Francisco, 1989.

Ellis, Roger and Chris Seaton, *New Celts*, Eastbourne, 1998.

Ferguson, Ronald, *Chasing the Wild Goose: the Story of the Iona Community*, second ed, Glasgow, 1998.

Finney, John, *Rediscovering the Past: Celtic and Roman Mission*, London, 1996.

Hamill, Jacynth, ed, *Travelling the Road of Faith: Worship Resources from the Corrymeela Community*, Belfast, 2001.

Heppenstall-West, Annie, *Reclaiming the Sealskin: Meditations on the Celtic Spirit*, Glasgow, 2002, 2004.

Iona Community Worship Book, Glasgow, 1988. Revised 1991 ('Grey Worship Book').

Iona Abbey Worship Book, Glasgow, 2001.

Iona Community: The Story of the Early Years: Oral History Project 2004-05, Glasgow. Unpublished.

Julian, Helen, *The Lindisfarne Icon: St Cuthbert and the 21st century Christian*, Oxford, 2004.

King, Chris, *Our Celtic Heritage. Looking at our own Faith in the Light of Celtic Christianity: a Study Guide for Christian Groups*, Edinburgh: Saint Andrews Press, 1997.

McIlhagga, Kate, *The Green Heart of the Snowdrop*, Glasgow, 2004.

Maclean, Alistair, *Hebridean Altars: The Spirit of an Island Race*, Edinburgh, 1937, London, 1999.

MacLeod, George, *The Whole Earth Shall Cry Glory*, Glasgow, 1985.

McMaster, Johnston, *The Future Returns: A journey with Columba and Augustine of Canterbury*, Corrymeela, 1997.

Marsh, William Parker and Christopher Bamford, *An anthology of Celtic Christianity*, Also titled, *Celtic Christianity: ecology and holiness: an anthology*, Edinburgh, 1986.

Miller, Peter, *An Iona Prayer Book*, Norwich, 1998.

Mitton, Michael, *Restoring the Woven Cord: Strands of Celtic Christianity for the Church Today*, London, 1995.

Monaghan, Patricia, ed, *Irish Spirit: Pagan, Celtic, Christian, Global*, Dublin, Wolfhound, 2001.

Newell, Philip, *Listening for the Heartbeat of God: a 'Celtic spirituality'*, London, 1997.

—, *One Foot in Eden: A Celtic View of the Stages of Life*, London, 1998.

Northumbria Community, *Celtic Daily Prayer*, London, 2005.

O'Donohue, John, *Anam Cara: Spiritual Wisdom from the Celtic World*, London, New York, Toronto, Sydney, Auckland, 1997, 1999.

—, *Eternal echoes: Exploring our hunger to belong*, London etc.1998.

—, *Conamara blues*, London etc. 2000.

—, *Benedictus*, London etc. 2007.

Ó Duinn, Seán, *Ag guí ar nós ár Sinsear*, BÁC (Dublín), 1984.

—, *Where Three Steams Meet*, Dublín, 2000, 2006.

O'Loughlin, Thomas, (2000b) *Journeys on the Edges: the Celtic Tradition*, London, 2000.

O'Malley, Brendan, *Celtic Blessings*, Norwich, 1998.

Ó Ríordáin, John, *The Music of What Happens: 'Celtic spirituality': a view from the Inside*, Dublin, 1996.

Olsen, Ted, *Christianity and the Celts*, Oxford, 2003.

Paynter, Neil, ed, *Gathered and Scattered: Readings and Meditations from the Iona Community*, Glasgow, 2007.

Reith, Martin, *God in Our midst*, London, 1975.

Robinson, Martin, *Rediscovering the Celts*, London, 2000.

Rodgers, Michael and Marcus Losack, *Glendalough: a Celtic Pilgrimage*, Dublin, 1996.

Rutherford, Alastair, *An Island Between Heaven and Earth*, BBC Radio 4 Play, 13 April 2004.

Sampson, Fay, *Visions and Voyages: the Story of our Celtic Heritage*, London, 1998.

Simpson, Ray, *Exploring 'Celtic spirituality': historical roots for our future*, London, 1995.

—, *Soul friendship: Celtic Insights into Spiritual Mentoring*, London, 1999.

—, *'Celtic spirituality': Rhythm, roots and relationships*, Cambridge, 2003.

— and The Community of Aidan and Hilda, *The Celtic Prayer Book*, Stowmarket, 2003.

Shanks, Norman, *Iona – God's Energy: the Spirituality and Vision of the Iona Community*, London, 1999.

Toulson, Shirley, *The Celtic Alternative: A Reminder of the Christianity We Lost*, London, 1987, 1990.

—, *The Celtic Year*, Element Books, 1996.

Tremayne, Peter [Peter Beresford-Ellis], *Absolution by Murder: A Sister Fidelma Mystery*, London 1994.

—, *Act of Mercy*, London, 1999.

Van de Weyer, Robert, *Celtic Fire: an Anthology of Celtic Christian Literature*, London, 1990.

—, *Celtic Gifts: Orders of Ministry in the Celtic Church*, Norwich, 1997.

Wallace, Martin, *The Celtic Resource Book*, London, 1998.

De Waal, Esther, *The Celtic Vision*, London, 1988.

—, *A World Made Whole: Rediscovering the Celtic Tradition*, London, 1991.

—, *The Celtic Way of Prayer: the Recovery of the Religious Imagination*, London, 1996.

—, *Every Earthly Blessing: Rediscovering the Celtic Tradition*, London, 1991, Harrisburg, 1999.

Wild Goose Worship Group, *A Wee Worship Book*, Glasgow, 1989. Fourth Incarnation, Glasgow, 1999.

4. WEBSITES REFERENCED

www.aidanandhilda.org.uk

www. iona.org

www.othona.org.

www.northumbriacommunity.org

5. OTHER WORKS CITED

Baptist Union of Great Britain, *Patterns and Prayers for Christian Worship*, Oxford, 1991.

Boswell, James, *Boswell's Journal of a Tour to the Hebrides*, eds Frederick A. Pottle and Charles H. Bennett, London, 1936.

Brooks, W. H. ed, *Pagan Review*. Issue 1, 1892.

Counsell, Michael, *2000 Years of Prayer*, Norwich, 1999.

Danagher, Kevin, *The Year in Ireland*, Cork, 1972.

Davey, Shaun, *The Pilgrim*, Dublin: Tara Music, 1983, rev c. 1992.

Duffy, Eamon, *The Stripping of the Altars: Traditional Religion in England 1400-1580*, New Haven/London, 1992.

Faith in the City. Report of the Archbishop's Commission on Urban Priority Areas, London, 1985.

Ferguson, Ronald, *Chasing the Wild Goose: The Story of the Iona Community*, London, 1988, Glasgow, 1998.

—, *George McLeod: Founder of the Iona Community*, London, 1990, Glasgow, 2001.

Fowler, James W., *Stages of Faith,* San Francisco, 1995.

Frazer, James, *The Golden Bough*, London 1890. Twelve volume edition, London 1906-15.

Gray, Nicholas Stuart, *The Seventh Swan*, 1962.

Hole, Christina, *A Dictionary of British Folk Customs*, London, 1976.

Jamieson, Alan, *A Churchless Faith*, London, 2002.

Johnson, Samuel, *A Journey to the Western Islands of Scotland,* ed Donal M'Nicol, Glasgow, 1817.

Martin, Martin, *A Description of the Western Isles of Scotland circa 1695*, Stirling, 1934.

MacArthur, Mairi, *That illustrious island: Iona through Travellers' Eyes*, Iona, 1991.

McCreary, Alf, *In War and Peace: the Story of Corrymeela*, Belfast, 2007.

MacLeod, George, *The Future of the Traditional Churches: Pentecostalism and Peace*, Glasgow, 1972.

Pococke, Richard, *Tours in Scotland 1747, 1750, 1760*, ed Daniel William Kemp, Edinburgh, 1887.

Severin, Tim, *The Brendan Voyage*, London, 1978.

Welch, Robert, *The Oxford Companion to Irish Literature*, Oxford, 1996.

Yeats, William Butler, *The Celtic Twilight*, London, 1893.